DIANA

Her True Story

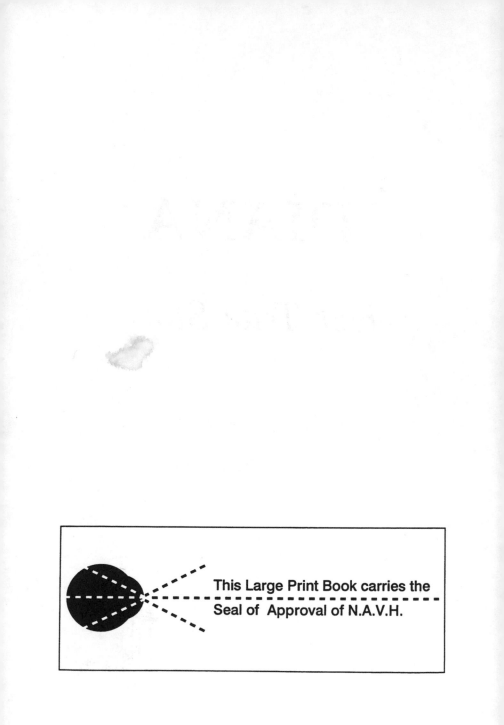

This Large Print Book carries the
Seal of Approval of N.A.V.H.

DIANA

Her True Story

ANDREW MORTON

Thorndike Press • Thorndike, Maine

Library of Congress Cataloging in Publication Data:

Morton, Andrew, 1953-
  Diana : her true story / Andrew Morton.
    p. cm.
  ISBN 1-56054-608-5 (alk. paper : lg. print)
  ISBN 1-56054-889-4 (alk. paper : lg. print : pbk.)
  1. Diana, Princess of Wales, 1961- . 2. Great
Britain—Princes and princesses—Biography. 3. Large type
books. I. Title.
  [DA591.A45M67   1993]   92-41519
  941.085'092—dc20   CIP
  [B]

Thorndike Large Print® Basic Series edition published in
1993 by arrangement with Simon & Schuster, Inc.

Cover design @ 1992 by Robert Anthony Inc.
Cover photo by Patrick Denarchelier.

The tree indicium is a trademark of Thorndike Press.

This book is printed on acid-free, high opacity paper. ∞

Contents

Photograph Acknowledgments

Before his death in March this year, the father of the Princess of Wales, the 8th Earl Spencer, very kindly allowed access to his private family photograph albums. Most of the photographs in this volume are reproduced from those albums. His generous cooperation is greatly appreciated.

The beautiful modern portraits of the Princess of Wales and her children which appear in this book are all by Patrick Demarchelier. It should be noted that Mr Demarchelier has donated all of his fees to the charity Turning Point.

The sources of all other photographs in this volume are stated in the captions.

Acknowledgments

The eternal problem facing royal writers is that of authenticity. How to convince the world of the truth of your account and the veracity of your sources when so many interviews are conducted on a confidential basis. The opposite problem afflicts those chosen by Buckingham Palace to write authorized stories of royal lives. While they have access to official archives, influential friends and members of the royal Household there is always, in the public mind, the lingering suspicion that even though they are being served the truth it is not necessarily the whole truth.

This biography of the Princess of Wales is unusual in that it is independent of control by Buckingham Palace and yet many of the Princess's family, friends and counsellors agreed to be interviewed, many of them for the first time, about her private and public life. They spoke with honesty and frankness in spite of the fact it meant laying aside the ingrained habits of discretion and loyalty which proximity to royalty invariably engenders. My thanks for their co-operation is therefore all the more heartfelt and sincere.

My grateful thanks too to the Princess of Wales's brother, the 9th Earl Spencer, for his insights and reminiscences, particularly about the Princess's childhood and teenage years.

My thanks also to the Baroness Falkender, Carolyn Bartholomew, Sue Beechey, Dr James Colthurst, James Gilbey, Malcolm Groves, Lucinda Craig Harvey, Peter and Neil Hickling, Felix Lyle, Michael Nash, Delissa Needham, Adam Russell, Rory Scott, Angela Serota, Muriel Stevens, Oonagh Toffolo and Stephen Twigg.

There are others whose present positions preclude them from being officially acknowledged for their invaluable assistance. Their unstinting guidance has been priceless.

My thanks to my publisher Michael O'Mara for his guidance and support on the tortuous path from conception to completion and to my wife Lynne for her patience and forbearance.

Andrew Morton
April 1992

1

"This Is Only the Beginning"

The voice on the other end of the telephone line was abrupt and filled with contained excitement. "Go to scrambler" it said. This was not the operations room of a naval warship or a secret room in the White House but my modest office above a restaurant in north London. The scrambler device was duly attached to the standard telephone and the first details emerged of Prince Charles's dismissal of his private secretary, Major-General Sir Christopher Airey.

That call, made from a windy public phone box on one of the most north-westerly islands in Europe, was the first step along the twisting path which led directly to the heart of the British monarchy. It set in motion an inquiry into the truth concerning the Princess of Wales, her marriage and her life within the royal family. It was to prove a salutary and startling education.

After a decade spent watching the workings of the modern monarchy, writing numerous books, and pontificating on TV and radio around the world about the royal family, I thought I had a solid knowledge of the subject. The last year has taught me how little I really knew about what goes on behind the wrought-iron gates of Buckingham Palace and the red brick walls of Kensington Palace.

I published the story about the dismissal in the *Sunday Times*. It was followed a week later by a longer piece which discussed the rivalry which exists between the offices of the Prince and the Princess of Wales. A few weeks later, at the time of Diana's 30th birthday, I wrote a further story about how Jimmy Savile, the television personality, had been instrumental in arranging a reconciliation between the royal couple following disclosures that Diana had refused her husband's offer of a birthday party at Highgrove.

The publication of these stories in the *Sunday Times* had several effects. First, they generated a witch hunt inside the palace to discover my sources. Long experience had told me that this was to be expected. Prince Charles's new private secretary, Commander Richard Aylard pored over the articles looking for clues while the Queen's private secretary, Sir Robert Fellowes pointed the finger at the staff inside Kensington Palace.

A terse phone call from Arthur Edwards, a long-serving photographer from *The Sun* newspaper, whose avuncular manner belies the fact that he has excellent sources inside the royal world, reinforced the message. "I didn't believe that Jimmy Savile stuff you wrote on Sunday," he said. "Then I spoke to one of my contacts and he said it was on the money. I'm just ringing to warn you: be careful, they are looking for your sources." [This message was dramatically reinforced in March this year when I broke the story about the impending separation of the Duke and Duchess of York. A call from a trusted contact informed me that senior police officers from the Royalty and Diplomatic Protection squad had been summoned to Buckingham Palace and ordered to find who leaked the story. "Watch your phones," I was brusquely cautioned. Ten days later my office was broken into.]

At the same time these original articles, which were generally sympathetic to the Princess of Wales, proved to those around her, many of whom I would meet later, that at last her side of the story could be told fairly. They were dismayed by the crop of books and articles which celebrated the 10th anniversary of the Waleses' marriage and Diana's 30th birthday. For the most part she was portrayed as a frivolous ingenue whose emotional and intellectual development was gently guided by her serious-minded husband. The general consensus was that, while their marriage may have had its ups and downs, they were now amicable companions pursuing separate interests but united by a common duty.

I was soon to learn that those closest to the Princess considered those sentiments to be a grotesque parody of the truth. A mid-week meeting with a member of Diana's circle in the incongruous circumstances of a working men's cafe in North Ruislip outside London was the turning point. As the tables around us tucked into bacon and eggs, an alarming story unfolded of the true nature of Diana's life inside Kensington Palace.

The facts, which spilled out in no particular order, revealed the flip side of the fairytale. In plain terms Diana believed Prince Charles was still seeing his girlfriend from before the marriage. She is Camilla Parker-Bowles, the wife of a member of the Queen's Household. At times she had hosted dinner parties at Highgrove with Charles and accompanied him on holidays. Over the years Diana had overheard their telephone conversations, had been aware of her affectionate correspondence with Charles, and watched with horrified fascination the way they behaved in public towards each other.

Amid the clatter of cutlery and crockery,

my contact revealed how Diana had seriously considered calling off the wedding two days before she walked down the aisle at St Paul's Cathedral. She discovered that Charles planned to give Camilla a bracelet inscribed with their nicknames "Fred" and "Gladys". She discovered the truth about their affectionate petnames a few weeks previously when Camilla was taken ill. On that occasion he sent her a bouquet of flowers, from "Fred" to "Gladys".

As a result Diana considered her wedding day to be one of the most emotionally confusing times of her life. On her honeymoon Diana saw photographs of Camilla fall out of his diary; later Charles appeared at dinner wearing cufflinks with two "C"s intertwined. He admitted they were a gift from the woman he once loved and lost. From this false start, their marriage had many more vicissitudes until it has now reached a point where they are barely on speaking terms.

The strain of her royal life and the reality of Diana's marriage has triggered a potentially fatal eating disorder, bulimia nervosa which has dogged her throughout her royal career. At times the loneliness of her position has brought her to the edge of despair, so much so that she has made a number of suicide attempts, some more half-hearted than others.

The dark ages, as she called them, have covered most of her royal life.

Yet the heartening aspect of her story was the way Diana had come to terms with her life and how, with the help of friends and counsellors, she was finding her true nature. The story of her transformation from victim to victor, a process that continues to this day, is the subject of this book.

A number of incidents, some more significant than others, brought about that change; a late night confrontation with Camilla Parker-Bowles; her behaviour following the avalanche in Klosters, Switzerland which nearly claimed her husband's life; comforting a grieving stranger in a Nottingham hospital, and deciding at last to seek treatment for her chronic eating disorder. During 1991 she became aware of just how much she had changed by her commitment to her friend Adrian Ward-Jackson when he was dying of AIDS. It was an experience which enriched her life, giving her a greater understanding of herself and a surer sense of purpose. The most obvious outward sign of the inner development was her new shorter hairstyle which signified the liberation she feels from her past life.

Clearly there was material here for a book which would radically revise the way the Princess of Wales was seen by the public. My pub-

14

lisher Michael O'Mara, a hard-nosed American from Pennsylvania, needed convincing. "If she was so miserable, why was she always smiling?" asked the man who had printed more pictures of Diana than any man alive. It did not help that the "Hitler Diaries", the story of how a forger fooled British and German newspapers as well as reputable historians with amateurish fakes purporting to be the German leader's handwritten diaries, was currently on television. O'Mara was deeply sceptical.

A meeting was arranged with my contacts and other interested parties. O'Mara listened to extracts from several tape recorded interviews, read certain documents and looked through a number of previously unpublished pictures. There was a long silence when the tape recorder was switched off. Drawing deeply on a Havana cigar, O'Mara said: "How in hell are we going to prove all this?"

That was the central problem. Much of the material which was then available could not, for reasons of confidentiality, be attributed. A strategy was finally agreed. Every aspect of this story had to be substantiated and amplified by interviews with family, friends and counsellors of the Princess of Wales. It was a task which occupied the next ten months. The one certain prediction made by her astrologer, Felix Lyle, as we discussed her life and character one balmy summer's evening in August 1991 was that it would be a tortuous path. How right he was. Meetings took place in various locations: near Diana's Gloucestershire home, in Hampshire and Dorset, in Scotland and even America. People who had kindly given assistance for earlier books, particularly *Inside Buckingham Palace* and *Duchess* were asked to help.

Secrecy was essential. The mandarins at Buckingham Palace like to control the flow of information concerning their royal principals. In this regard they are no different from any other large organization. Those authors who operate independently of Palace purview soon discover that doors are quickly locked, bolted and barred to inquiry.

However, once a number of additional begging letters — requests for interviews — were sent, it became apparent that there were a substantial number of Diana's "inner circle" who felt it was time to set her record straight. They believed that for once the truth should be told about the difficult life Diana has led and, for the most part, still leads. These taped interviews, most on the record, others unattributable, amply endorsed the original premise. One close friend explained why so many of her circle had decided to co-operate. He said:

"For ten years we have sat and watched Diana being destroyed. We've often spoken about her and said that something has got to happen. But nothing has. It was painful for us all to see a delightful candle being progressively snuffed out by the royal system and an empty marriage."

This was an undercover operation which had to be conducted with great speed as it quickly emerged that there was every chance that the Princess might well have left the royal circle by the proposed September publication date of the book. As James Gilbey, a member of the distilling dynasty who has known Diana since she was 17, noted: "She said to me recently that she hadn't made any date in her diary past July because she doesn't think she is going to be there." Her dramatic assertion may have been wish fulfillment, a hyperbolic statement expressing her real desires, but with such an unstable outlook we couldn't take any chances: publication was brought forward to June. In view of the Duchess of York's abrupt departure from the royal family in March this year it was a prudent decision.

As the interviews progressed, a very distinct new picture of Diana surfaced from beneath the highly varnished image. Behind the public smiles Diana is a lonely and unhappy young woman who endures a loveless marriage, is seen as an outsider by the Queen and the rest of the royal family and is frequently at odds with the aims and objectives of the pervasive royal system. As Oonagh Toffolo, who once nursed the Duke of Windsor and regularly visits Diana for sessions of acupuncture and meditation, observes: "She is a prisoner of the system just as surely as any woman incarcerated in Holloway jail."

Amid the cloud of silver photo frames, the clutter of Herend porcelain and other knick-knacks which Diana collects and displays in her private rooms at Kensington Palace is a shredder to destroy her mail and a telephone scrambler to disguise her private calls. Last summer she had her rooms secretly "swept" with an electronic gadget to seek out any possible bugging device. It was clean but the doubts remain. She even exercises extreme caution about what she throws into her wastepaper bin. No one and nothing can be trusted.

There is no doubt she feels that she has paid a high price for her royal life and looks forward to the day when she can spend a weekend in Paris or, as she says, "I can run along a beach without a policeman following me." As she dreams and hopes, she endures a marriage and a position which has yielded meagre satisfaction and much pain. While she is now

18

more in control of herself and her life, her fate hangs in the balance.

She endlessly debates the central dilemma in her life. If she divorces Prince Charles she loses her children and the chance to use her special gifts to help those in need, whether it be the homeless, AIDS patients or victims of leprosy. If she stays she is trapped in a marriage and lifestyle which offers scant prospect of achieving personal happiness. As her best friend, Carolyn Bartholomew observes of the woman she has known since they were schoolgirls: "She is not a happy person but she once was and it is my dearest hope that one day she will find the happiness she truly deserves."

While she occupies an isolated public position she has drawn great comfort from her two children, Princes William and Harry, who are undoubtedly the two most important people in her life. They are her stalwart supporters in a closed, oppressive world.

Over-protective, in the way that single parents are, she lavishes them with love, cuddles and affection. "Who loves you most?" is a favourite phrase as she tucks them up in bed or tousles their hair. She loves them unconditionally and absolutely, determined to ensure that they do not suffer the same kind of childhood she did, where she wanted for nothing materially but everything emotionally.

As she says: "I want to bring them up with security, not to anticipate things because they will be disappointed. That's made my own life so much easier. I hug my children to death and get into bed with them at night. I always feed them love and affection. It's so important."

While she knows that Prince William will one day become king she is firm in her belief that she will never become queen. This profound sense of destiny which has influenced her life gives her an intuitive awareness that she has been singled out for a special role. Her fate has taken her on a different journey, a route where the monarchy is secondary to her true vocation.

That road leads inexorably to her work for the sick, the dying and the distressed. The inner spiritual resources which sustained and nourished her in her darkest hours are now manifested in her uncanny empathy with those in need. It is a calling. As her brother, the 9th Earl Spencer, told me: "She strikes me as an immensely Christian figure and she has the strength which I think true Christians have and the direction in her life which others can envy; that sureness of her purpose and the strength of her character and position to do an enormous amount of good. I am sure she will continue to do so."

The irony of her life is that if she had enjoyed a happy marriage these qualities may have remained dormant. The private work she has undertaken in bereavement counselling and nursing the terminally ill has given her intense fulfillment. "I love it, I can't wait to get into it. It's like a hunger," she says.

She has suffered much in the last decade but that experience has given her the inner fortitude to shoulder the emotional burden she must carry on the next stage of her life's journey. As Mother Teresa told her during her visit to Rome this year: "To heal other people you have to suffer yourself." Diana nodded vigorously in agreement.

While she struggles to find an acceptable equilibrium in her life, she acknowledges the progress she has made. She says: "I've opened up. My life is changing. This is only the beginning."

2

"I Was Supposed to Be a Boy"

It is a memory indelibly engraved upon her soul. Diana Spencer sat quietly at the bottom of the cold stone stairs at her Norfolk home, clutching the wrought-iron banisters while all around her there was a determined bustle. She could hear her father loading suitcases into the boot of a car, then Frances, her mother, crunching across the gravel forecourt, the clunk of the car door being shut and the sound of a car engine revving and then slowly fading as her mother drove through the gates of Park House and out of her life. Diana was six years old. A quarter of a century later, it is a moment she can still picture in her mind's eye and she can still summon up the painful feelings of rejection, breach of trust and isolation that the break-up of her parents' marriage signified to her.

It may have happened differently but that is the picture Diana carries with her. There are many other snapshots of her childhood which crowd her memory. Her mother's tears, her father's lonely silences, the numerous nannies she resented, the endless shuttling between parents, the sound of her brother Charles sobbing himself to sleep, the feelings of guilt that she wasn't born a boy and the firmly fixed idea that somehow she was a "nuisance" to have around. She craved cuddles and kisses; she was given a catalogue from Hamley's toy shop. It was a childhood where she wanted for nothing materially but everything emotionally. "She comes from a privileged background but she had a childhood that was very hard," says her astrologer Felix Lyle.

The Honourable Diana Spencer was born late on the afternoon of July 1, 1961, the third daughter of Viscount Althorp, then aged 37, and Viscountess Althorp, 12 years his junior. She weighed 7lb 12oz and while her father expressed his delight at a "perfect physical specimen" there was no hiding the sense of anticlimax, if not downright disappointment, in the family that the new arrival was not the longed-for-male heir who would carry on the Spencer name. Such was the anticipation of a boy that the couple hadn't considered any girls' names. A week later they settled on "Diana Frances", after the infant's mother and a Spencer ancestress.

While Viscount Althorp, the late Earl Spencer, may have been proud of his new daughter — Diana was very much the apple of his eye — his remarks about her health could have been chosen more diplomatically. Just eighteen months previously Diana's mother had given birth to John, a baby so badly deformed and sickly that he survived for only ten hours. It was a harrowing time for the couple and there was much pressure from older members of the family to see "what was wrong with the mother". They wanted to know why she kept producing girls. Lady Althorp, still only 23, was sent to various Harley Street clinics in London for intimate tests. For Diana's mother, fiercely proud, combative and tough-minded, it was a humiliating and unjust experience, all the more so in retrospect as nowadays it is known that the sex of the baby is determined by the man. As her son Charles, the new Earl Spencer, observes: "It was a dreadful time for my parents and probably the root of their divorce because I don't think they ever got over it."

While she was too young to understand, Diana certainly caught the pitch of the family's frustration, and, believing that she was "a nuisance", she accepted a corresponding load of guilt and failure for disappointing her parents and family, feelings she has now learned to accept and recognize.

Three years after Diana's birth the longed-for son arrived. Unlike Diana who was christened in Sandringham church and had well-to-do commoners for godparents, baby brother Charles was christened in style at Westminster Abbey with the Queen as principal godparent. The infant was heir to a rapidly diminishing but still substantial fortune accumulated in the fifteenth century when the Spencers were among the wealthiest sheep traders in Europe. With their fortune they collected an earldom from Charles I, built Althorp House in Northamptonshire, acquired a family crest and motto — "God defend the right" — and amassed a fine collection of art, antiques, books and *objets d'art*.

For the next three centuries Spencers were at home in the palaces of Kensington, Buckingham and Westminster as they occupied various offices of State and Court. If a Spencer never quite reached the commanding heights, they certainly walked confidently along the corridors of power. Spencers became Knights of the Garter, Privy Councillors, ambassadors and a First Lord of the Admiralty while the third Earl Spencer was considered as a possible Prime Minister. They were linked by blood to Charles II, the Dukes of Marlborough, Devonshire and Abercorn and through a quirk of history to seven American presidents, including Franklin D. Roosevelt, and to the actor Humphrey Bogart and, it is said, the gangster Al Capone.

The Spencer qualities of quiet public service, the values of *noblesse oblige* were well expressed in their service to the Sovereign. Generations of Spencer men and women have fulfilled the functions of Lord Chamberlain, equerry, lady-in-waiting and other positions at Court. Diana's paternal grandmother, Countess Spencer was a Lady of the Bedchamber to Queen Elizabeth, the Queen Mother, while her maternal grandmother, Ruth, Lady Fermoy, is currently one of her Women of the Bedchamber, a position she has held for nearly thirty years. The late Earl Spencer served as equerry to both King George VI and the present Queen.

However, it was the family of Diana's mother, the Fermoys, with their roots in Ireland and connections in the United States, who were responsible for the acquisition of Park House, her childhood home in Norfolk. As a mark of friendship with his second son, the Duke of York (later George VI), King George V granted Diana's grandfather, Maurice Fermoy, the 4th Baron, the lease of Park House, a spacious property originally built to accommodate the overflow of guests and staff from nearby Sandringham House.

The Fermoys certainly made a mark on the

area. Maurice Fermoy became the Conservative Member of Parliament for King's Lynn while his Scottish wife, who gave up a promising career as a concert pianist to marry, founded the King's Lynn Festival for Arts and Music which, since its inception in 1951, has attracted world renowned musicians such as Sir John Barbirolli and Yehudi Menuhin.

For the young Diana Spencer, this long noble heritage was not so much impressive as terrifying. She never relished visits to the ancestral home of Althorp. There were too many creepy corners and badly lit corridors peopled with portraits of long-dead ancestors whose eyes followed her unnervingly. As her brother recalls: "It was like an old man's club with masses of clocks ticking away. For an impressionable child it was a nightmarish place. We never looked forward to going there."

This sense of foreboding was hardly helped by the bad-tempered relationship which existed between her gruff grandfather Jack, the 7th Earl, and his son Johnnie Althorp. For many years they were barely on grunting, let alone speaking terms. Abrupt to the point of rudeness yet fiercely protective of Althorp, Diana's grandfather earned the nickname of "the curator earl" because he knew the history of every picture and piece of furniture in his stately home. He was so proud of his domain that he often followed visitors around with a duster and once, in the library, snatched a cigar from out of Winston Churchill's mouth. Beneath this irascible veneer was a man of cultivation and taste, whose priorities contrasted sharply with his son's *laissez-faire* approach to life and amiable enjoyment of the traditional outdoor pursuits of an English country gentleman.

While Diana was in awe of her grandfather, she adored her grandmother, Countess Spencer. "She was sweet, wonderful and very special. Divine really," says the Princess. The Countess was known locally for her frequent visits to the sick and the infirm and never at a loss for a generous word or gesture. While Diana has inherited her mother's sparky, strong-willed nature she has also been blessed with her paternal grandmother's qualities of thoughtfulness and compassion.

In contrast to the eerie splendours of Althorp, Diana's rambling ten-bedroomed home, Park House, was positively cosy notwithstanding the staff cottages, extensive garages, outdoor swimming pool, tennis court and cricket pitch in the grounds as well as the six full-time staff who included a cook, a butler and a private governess.

Screened from the road by trees and shrubs,

the house is substantial but its dirty, sand-brick exterior makes it appear rather bleak and lonely. In spite of its forbidding appearance, the Spencer children loved the rambling pile. When they moved to Althorp in 1975 on the death of their grandfather, the 7th Earl, Charles said goodbye to every room and Diana today still revisits her former home, even though it has been turned into a Cheshire Home holiday hotel for the disabled.

Park House was a home of atmosphere and great character. On the ground floor was the stone-flagged kitchen, the dark green laundry room, domain of Diana's foul-tempered ginger cat called Marmalade, and the schoolroom where their governess, Miss Gertrude Allen — known as "Ally" — taught the girls the rudiments of reading and writing. Next door was what the children called "The Beatle Room", a room devoted entirely to psychedelic posters, pictures and other memorabilia of the Sixties' pop stars. It was a rare concession to the postwar era. Elsewhere the house was a snapshot of upper-class English life, decorated with formal family portraits, regimental pictures, as well as the plaques, photographs and certificates which were testimony of a lifetime spent in good works.

From her pretty cream bedroom in the first floor nursery, Diana enjoyed a pleasant prospect of grazing cattle, a patchwork of open fields and parkland interspersed with copses of pine, silver birch and yew. Rabbits, foxes and other woodland creatures were regularly seen on the lawns while the frequent sea frets which softly curled around her sash windows were evidence that the Norfolk coast was only six miles away.

It was a heavenly place for growing children. They fed trout in the lake at Sandringham House, slid down the banisters, took Jill, their springer spaniel, for long rambles, played hide and seek in the garden, listened to the wind whistling through the trees and hunted for pigeons' eggs. In summer they swam in the heated outdoor swimming pool, looked for frogs and newts, picnicked on the beach near their private hut at Brancaster and played in their very own tree house. And, as in Enid Blyton's Famous Five children's books, there was always "lashings of ginger beer" and the smell of something appetizing baking in the kitchen.

Like her elder sisters, Diana was on horseback at three and soon developed a passion for animals, the smaller the better. She had pet hamsters, rabbits, guinea pigs, her cat Marmalade, which Charles and Jane loathed, and, as her mother recalls, "anything in a small cage". When one of her menagerie died, Diana dutifully performed a burial ceremony. While goldfish were flushed down the toilet, she normally placed her other dead pets in a cardboard shoe box, dug a hole beneath the spreading cedar tree on the lawn and laid them to rest. Finally, she placed a makeshift cross above their grave.

Graveyards held a sombre fascination. Charles and Diana frequently visited their brother John's lichen-covered grave in the Sandringham churchyard and mused about what he would have been like and whether they would have been born if he had lived. Charles feels that his parents would have completed their family with Diana while the Princess herself feels that she would not have been born. It was a matter for endless unresolved conjecture. In Diana's young mind her brother's gravestone, with its simple "In Loving Memory" epitaph, was a permanent reminder that, as she now recalls: "I was the girl who was supposed to be a boy."

Just as her childhood amusements could have originated from the pages of a 1930s' children's book, so Diana's upbringing reflected the values of a bygone age. She had a nanny, Kent-born Judith Parnell, who took the infant Diana for walks around the grounds in a well-used, highly-sprung perambulator. Indeed, Diana's first memory is "the smell of the warm plastic" of her pram hood. The growing girl did not see as much of her mother as she would have wished and less of her father. Her sisters Sarah and Jane, her senior by six and four years respectively, were already spending mornings in the downstairs classroom when she was born and by the time Diana was ready to join them they were packing their bags for boarding-school.

Mealtimes were spent with nanny. Simple fare was the order of the day. Cereals at breakfast, mince and vegetables for lunch and fish every Friday. Her parents were a benign though distant presence and it wasn't until Charles was seven that he actually sat down to a meal with his father in the downstairs dining-room. There was a formality and restraint to their childhood, a reflection of the way Diana's parents were raised. As Charles recalls: "It was a privileged upbringing out of a different age, a distant way of living from your parents. I don't know anyone who brings up children like that any more. It certainly lacked a mother figure."

Privileged yes, snobbish no. At a very early age the Spencer children had impressed upon them the value of good manners, honesty and accepting people for what they are, not for their position in life. Charles says: "We never understood the whole title business. I didn't even know I had any kind of title until I went to prep school when I started to get these letters saying: 'The Honourable Charles'. Then I started to wonder what it was all about. We had no idea that we were privileged. As children we accepted our circumstances as normal."

Their royal next-door neighbours simply fitted in to a social landscape of friends and acquaintances who included the children of the Queen's land agent, Charles and Alexandra Loyd, the local vicar's daughter Penelope Ashton, and William and Annabel Fox, whose mother Carol was Diana's godmother. Social relations with the royal family were sporadic, especially as they only spend a small part of the year on their 20,000-acre estate. A royal visit to Park House was such a rare event that when Princess Anne said she would call round after church service one Sunday there was consternation in the Althorp household. Diana's father didn't drink and staff frantically searched through the cupboards looking for a bottle of something suitable to offer their royal guest. Finally they found a cheap bottle of sherry, which had been won in a church bazaar, lying forgotten in a drawer.

Occasionally Princess Margaret's son, Viscount Linley, and the Princes Andrew and Edward might come to play for the afternoon but there certainly weren't the comings and goings many have assumed. In fact the Spencer children viewed their invitations to the Queen's winter home with trepidation. After watching a screening of the Walt Disney film, *Chitty, Chitty, Bang, Bang* in the private cinema, Charles had nightmares about a character called the Children Catcher. For Diana it was the "strange" atmosphere of Sandringham itself which she hated. On one occasion she refused to go. She kicked and screamed her defiance until her father told her that it would be considered very bad manners if she didn't join the other children. If anyone had told her then that one day she would join the royal family she would have run a mile.

If the atmosphere at Sandringham was uncomfortable, at Park House it became unbearable as Diana's little world fell apart at the seams. In September 1967 Sarah and Jane went to boarding-school at West Heath in Kent, a move which coincided with the collapse of the Althorps' 14-year marriage.

That summer they decided on a trial separation, a decision which came as a "thunderbolt, a terrible shock" to Charles, horrified both families and shocked the county set. Even for a family with a penchant for turning a drama into a crisis, this was an exceptional event. They remembered how their marriage in 1954 was trumpeted as "the society wedding of the year", their union endorsed by the presence of the Queen and Queen Mother. Certainly in his bachelor days Johnnie Spencer was the catch of the county. Not only was he heir to the Spencer estates, he also served with distinction as a captain in the Royal Scots Greys during World War Two and, as Equerry to the Queen, he had accompanied the Queen and Prince Philip on their historic tour of Australia shortly before his marriage.

The sophistication exuded by a man twelve years her senior was no doubt part of the attraction for the Honourable Frances Roche, the daughter of the 4th Baron Fermoy, who was an 18-year-old debutante when they first met. With her trim figure, vivacious personality and love of sports Frances caught the eye of many young men that season, among them Major Ronald Ferguson, the Duchess of York's father. However, it was Johnnie Spencer who won her heart and, after a short courtship, they married at Westminster Abbey in June 1954.

They obviously took the words of the Bishop of Norwich to heart. Just nine months after he declared: "You are making an addition to the home life of your country on which above all others, our national life depends," their first daughter Sarah was born. They settled for a country life; Johnnie studied at the Royal Agricultural College in Cirencester and, following an uneasy spell on the Althorp estate, they moved to Park House. Over the next few years they built up a 650-acre farm, a sizeable chunk of which was bought with £20,000 ($34,000) of Frances' inheritance.

Tensions soon simmered beneath the impression of domestic harmony and marital bliss. The pressure to produce a male heir was everpresent and there was Frances' growing realization that a lifestyle which had seemed urbane to her in her youth was, on mature reflection, dull and uninspiring. The late Earl Spencer said: "How many of those fourteen years were happy? I thought all of them, until the moment we parted. I was wrong. We hadn't fallen apart, we'd drifted apart."

As cracks appeared in the facade of unity, the atmosphere at Park House soured. In public the couple were all smiles, in private it was a different story. While the freezing silences, heated exchanges and bitter words can only be imagined, the traumatic effect on the children is only too evident. Diana clearly remembers witnessing a particularly violent argument between her mother and father as she peeked from her hiding-place behind the drawing-room door.

The catalyst which provoked that indignation was the appearance in their lives of a wealthy businessman, Peter Shand Kydd, who had recently returned to Britain after selling a sheep farm in Australia. The Althorps first met the extrovert university-educated entrepreneur and his artist wife, Janet Munro Kerr at a dinner party in London. A subsequent arrangement to go on a skiing holiday in Switzerland together proved a fatal turning point in their lives. Peter, an amusing *bon viveur* with an attractive bohemian streak, seemed to possess all the qualities Johnnie lacked. In the exhilaration of their affair Lady Althorp, eleven years his junior, did not notice his bouts of depression and black moods. That would come later.

On their return from holiday Peter, then aged 42, moved out of his London home leaving behind his wife and three children. At the same time he began to see Frances secretly at an address in South Kensington in central London.

When the Althorps agreed to a trial separation, Diana's mother moved out of Park House into a rented apartment in Cadogan Place, Belgravia. It was then that the myth of "the bolter" was born, that Frances had left her husband and deserted her four children for the love of another man. She was cast as the selfish villainess of the drama, her husband the innocent injured party. In fact when she left home Lady Althorp had already made arrangements for Charles and Diana to live with her in London. Diana was enrolled at a girls' day-school, Charles at a nearby kindergarten.

When Frances arrived at her new home, to be followed weeks later by her children and their nanny, she had every hope that the children would be relatively unaffected by her marital breakdown, especially as Sarah and Jane were away at boarding-school. During term-time the younger children returned to Park House at weekends while their father, Viscount Althorp, stayed with them in Belgravia when he visited London. They were bleak meetings. Charles's earliest memory is playing quietly on the floor with a train set while his mother sat sobbing on the edge of the bed, his father smiling weakly at him in a forlorn attempt to reassure his son that everything was all right. The family was reunited at Park House for half term and again during the Christmas holidays. But, as Mrs Shand Kydd has stated: "It was my last Christmas there for by now it had become apparent that the marriage had completely broken down."

That fateful visit was marked by a distinct absence of seasonal goodwill or tidings of joy for the future. Viscount Althorp insisted, against his wife's fierce objections, that the children return permanently to Park House and continue their education at Silfield school in King's Lynn. "He refused to let them return in the New Year to London," she said.

As the legal machinery for divorce ground into action, the children became pawns in a bitter and acrimonious battle which turned mother against daughter and husband against wife. Lady Althorp sued for custody of the children, an action started with every hope of success as the mother usually wins — unless the father is a nobleman. His rank and title give him prior claims.

The case, which was heard in June 1968, wasn't helped by the fact that two months earlier Lady Althorp had been named as the "other woman" in the Shand Kydds' divorce while most galling of all, her own mother, Ruth, Lady Fermoy, sided against her. It was the greatest betrayal of her life and one she will never forgive. The Althorps' divorce went through in April 1969 and a month later on May 2, Peter Shand Kydd and Lady Althorp married in a quiet register office ceremony and bought a house on the West Sussex coast where Peter could indulge his love of sailing.

It was not just the adults who were scarred by this vicious legal battle. However much their parents and the family tried to muffle the blow, the impact on the children was still profound. Subsequently, family friends and biographers have tried to minimize the effect. They have claimed that Sarah and Jane were barely troubled by the divorce as they were away at school, that Charles, aged four, was too young to understand while Diana, then seven, reacted to the break up with "the unthinking resilience of her age" or even regarded it as "fresh excitement" in her young life.

The reality was more traumatic than many have realized. It is significant that at one time in their lives both Sarah and Diana have suffered from debilitating eating disorders, anorexia nervosa and bulimia respectively. These illnesses are rooted in a complex web of relations between mother and daughter, food and anxiety and, to use the jargon, "malfunctioning" family life. As Diana says: "My parents were busy sorting themselves out. I remember my mother crying, daddy never spoke to us about it. We could never ask questions. Too many nannies. The whole thing was very unstable."

To the casual visitor Diana seemed happy enough. She was always a busy, tidy little girl, going around the house at night making sure all the curtains were drawn and tucking up the zoo of small furry animals which crowded her bed — she has kept them to this day. She raced around the driveway on her blue tricycle, took her dolls for walks in her pram — she always asked for a new one as a birthday present — and helped to dress her smaller brother. The warm, maternal, caring streak which has characterized her adult life, was becoming evident in her daily life. There were more frequent visits to grandparents and other relations. Countess Spencer often stayed at Park House while Ruth, Lady Fermoy taught the children card games. In her elegant home, described as "a little corner of Belgravia in Norfolk", she explained the intricacies of mah-jongg and bridge. However, there was no disguising the bewilderment Diana felt.

Night-times were worst. As children, Diana and Charles were afraid of the dark and they insisted that the landing light was left on or a candle lit in their rooms. With the wind whistling in the trees outside her window and the night-time cries of owls and other creatures, Park House could be a creepy place for a child. One evening when their father casually mentioned that a murderer was on the loose in the vicinity, the children were too terrified to sleep, listening anxiously to every rattle, creak and squeak in the silent house. Diana daubed luminous paint on the eyes of her cuddly green hippo so that at night it seemed as

41

though he was keeping watch and looking after her.

Every night as she lay in her bed, surrounded by her cuddly toys, she could hear her brother sobbing, crying for his mother. Sometimes she went to him, sometimes her fear of the dark overcame her maternal instincts and she stayed in her room listening as Charles wailed: "I want my mummy, I want my mummy." Then she too would bury her head in the pillow and weep. "I just couldn't bear it," she recalls. "I could never pluck up enough courage to get out of bed. I remember it to this day."

Nor did she have much confidence in many of the nannies who now worked at Park House. They changed with alarming frequency and ranged from the sweet to the sadistic. One nanny was sacked on the spot when Diana's mother discovered that her employee was lacing her elder daughters' food with laxatives as a punishment. She wondered why they constantly complained of stomach pains until she caught the woman redhanded.

Another nanny beat Diana on the head with a wooden spoon if she was naughty or alternatively banged Charles and Diana's heads together. Charles recalls kicking a hole in his bedroom door when he was sent to his room for no good reason. "Children have a natural sense of justice and if we felt they were unjust we would rebel," he explains. Other nannies, such as Sally Percival, now married and living in Northampton, were kind and sympathetic and still receive Christmas cards from the children today.

However, the task of a new nanny was made all the more difficult because the children, bewildered and unhappy, felt that they had come to take the place of their mother. The prettier they were, the more suspicious Diana was of them. They put pins in their chairs, threw their clothes out of the window and locked them in the bathroom. In fact Charles's childhood experiences confirmed him in his decision not to employ a nanny for his own children.

Their father sometimes joined the children for tea in the nursery but, as former nanny Mary Clarke recalls, "It was very hard going. In those early days he wasn't very relaxed with them." Johnnie buried himself in his work for Northamptonshire County Council, the National Association of Boys' Clubs and his cattle farm. His son recalls: "He was really miserable after the divorce, basically shell-shocked. He used to sit in his study the whole time. I remember occasionally, very occasionally, he used to play cricket with me on the lawn. That was a great treat."

School simply cast the problem in another mould. Charles and Diana were "different" and knew it. They were the only pupils at Silfield school whose parents were divorced. It set them apart from the start. A point emphasized by her former form captain, Delissa Needham: "She was the only girl I knew whose parents were divorced. Those things just didn't happen then."

The school itself was welcoming and friendly enough. Run by headmistress Jean Lowe, who gave evidence on Lord Althorp's behalf during the divorce case, it had a real family atmosphere. Classes were small and teachers were generous with house points and gold stars for achievements in reading, writing or drawing. Outside was a tennis court, a sandpit, a lawn for playing netball and rounders as well as a garden for weekly "scavenger hunts". Diana, unused to the hurly burly of school life, was quiet and shy although she did have her friend, Alexandra Loyd to keep her company.

While her handwriting was clear and she read fluently, Diana found the scholarly side rather confusing. Miss Lowe remembers her kindness to the smaller children, her love of animals and general helpfulness but not her academic potential. She was good at art as well but her friends couldn't explain why she burst into tears for no apparent reason during a painting class one sunny afternoon. They do remember that she dedicated all her pictures to "Mummy and Daddy".

As she muddled through her "tables" and *Janet and John* books, Diana became increasingly envious of her younger brother, who was remembered as a "solemn" but well-behaved little boy. "I longed to be as good as him in the schoolroom," she says. As with all siblings there were fights which Diana, being bigger and stronger, invariably won. And she pinched, Charles complained. Soon he realized that he could wound with words, teasing his sister mercilessly. Both parents ordered him to stop calling his sister "Brian", a nickname derived from a slow and rather dull-witted snail who featured in a popular children's TV show, "The Magic Roundabout".

He had sweet revenge with the unexpected help of the local vicar's wife. Charles says, with relish: "I don't know whether a pyschologist would say it was the trauma of the divorce but she had real difficulty telling the truth purely because she liked to embellish things. On the school run one day the vicar's wife stopped the car and said: 'Diana Spencer, if you tell one more lie like that I am going to make you walk home.' Of course I was triumphant because she had been rumbled."

While the sibling competition was an inevitable part of growing-up, far less bearable was the growing parental rivalry, conscious or not, as Frances and Johnnie vied with each other to win the love of their children. Yet while they showered their offspring with expensive presents this wasn't accompanied by the affectionate cuddles and kisses that the children craved. Diana's father, who already had a reputation locally for organizing splendid fireworks' displays on Guy Fawkes Night, laid on a wonderful party for her seventh birthday. He borrowed a camel called Bert from Dudley zoo and watched with evident delight as the surprised children were taken for rides around the lawn.

Christmas was simply an exercise in extravagance. Before the big day Charles and Diana were given the catalogue for Hamley's, a large toy store in London's West End, and told to pick what presents they wanted Father Christmas to bring. Lo and behold, on Christmas Day their wishes came true, the stockings on the end of their beds bulging with goodies. "It makes you very materialistic," says Charles. There was one present which gave Diana the most agonizing decision of her young life. In 1969 she was a guest at the wedding of her cousin, Elizabeth Wake-Walker and Anthony Duckworth-Chad held at St

James's Piccadilly. Her father gave her a smart blue dress, her mother an equally smart green dress. "I can't remember to this day which one I wore but I remember being totally traumatized by it because it would show favouritism."

That tightrope was walked every weekend when Charles and Diana took the train with their nanny from Norfolk to Liverpool Street station in London where their mother met them. Shortly after they reached her apartment in Belgravia the standard procedure was for their mother to burst into tears. "What's the matter, mummy?" they would chorus to which she invariably answered: "I don't want you to go tomorrow." It was a ritual which resulted in the children feeling guilty and confused. Holidays, split between parents, were just as grim.

In 1969 life became more relaxed and carefree when Peter Shand Kydd was officially introduced into their lives. They first met him on the platform at Liverpool Street station during one of their regular Friday shuttles between Norfolk and London. Handsome, smiling and smartly suited, he was an immediate hit, all the more so when their mother told them that they had been married that morning.

Peter, who made his fortune in the family

wallpaper business, was a generous, demon-strative and easy-going stepfather. After a brief time in Buckinghamshire, the newly-weds moved into an unassuming suburban house called Appleshore in Itchenor on the West Sussex coast where Peter, a Royal Navy veteran, took the children sailing. He allowed Charles to wear his admiral's hat and so his nickname "The Admiral" was born. Diana he dubbed "The Duchess", a nickname her friends still use. As Charles observes: "If you want an insight into why Diana is not just some sort of spoilt toff it is because we had very contrasting lifestyles. It wasn't all stately homes and butlers. My mother's home was an ordinary set up and every holiday we spent half our holiday with our mother so we were in an environment of relative normality for much of our time."

Three years later in 1972 the Shand Kydds bought a 1,000-acre farm on the isle of Seil, south of Oban in Argyllshire where Mrs Shand Kydd lives today. When the children came for summer holidays they enjoyed a "Swallows and Amazon" idyll, spending their days mack-erel fishing, lobster potting and sailing and, on fine days, enjoying barbeques on the beach. Diana even had her own Shetland pony called Souffle.

It was on horseback that she suffered a broken arm which has made her anxious about riding ever since. She was galloping on her pony, Romilly, in the grounds of Sandringham Park when the horse stumbled and she fell off. Although she was in pain, there was no evidence that the arm was broken and so two days later she went skiing to Switzerland. During the holiday her arm felt so lifeless that she went to a local Swiss hospital for an X-ray. She was diagnosed as suffering from "greenstick", a childhood condition where children's bones are so flexible that they bend, not break. A doctor strapped the arm but when she later tried to go riding again she lost her nerve and dismounted. She still rides but prefers to exercise by swimming or tennis because, living in central London, it is more convenient.

Swimming and dancing are also activities at which she excels. They stood her in good stead when her father enrolled her at her next school, Riddlesworth Hall, two hours' drive from Park House. She learned to love the school which tried to be a home away from home to the 120 girls. However, her first feelings when she was sent there were of betrayal and resentment. Diana was nine and felt the wrench from her father keenly. In her motherly concerned way, she was cosseting him as he tried to pick up the pieces of his life. His decision to send her away from her home and brother into an alien world was interpreted as rejection. She made threats like: "If you love me, you won't leave me here" as her father gently explained the benefits of attending a school which offered ballet, swimming, riding and a place to keep her beloved Peanuts, her guinea pig. She had won the Fur and Feather Section with him at the Sandringham Show — "Maybe that was because he was the only entry," she observes drily — and later won the Palmer Cup for Pets' Corner at her new school.

Her father also told her that she would be among friends. Alexandra Loyd, her cousin Diana Wake-Walker and Claire Pratt, the daughter of her godmother Sarah Pratt, were also at the all-girls' boarding-school near Diss in Norfolk. Nonetheless as he left her behind with her trunk labelled "D. Spencer", clutching her favourite green hippo — girls were only allowed one cuddly toy in bed — and Peanuts, he felt a deep sense of loss. "That was a dreadful day," he says, "dreadful losing her."

An excellent amateur cameraman, he took a photograph of her before she left home. It shows a sweet-faced girl, shy, yet with a sunny, open disposition, dressed in the school uniform which consisted of a dark red jacket and grey, pleated skirt. He saved too the note she sent requesting "Big choc. cake, ginger biscuits, Twiglets" just as he has kept the clipping she sent him from the *Daily Telegraph* about academic failures who become gifted and successful later in life.

Although quiet and demure in her first term she was no goody goody. She preferred laughter and skylarks to solid endeavour and while she could be noisy she shied away from being the centre of attention. Diana would never shout out answers in class or volunteer to read the lessons at assembly. Far from it. In one of her first school plays where she played a Dutch doll, Diana only agreed to take the part if she could remain silent.

Noisy with her friends in the dormitory, she was quiet in class. She was a popular pupil but somehow she always felt that she was set apart. Diana no longer felt so different because of her parents' divorce but because a voice inside her told her that she would be separate from the herd. That intuition told her that her life was, as she says, "going to be a winding road. I always felt very detached from everyone else. I knew I was going somewhere different, that I was in the wrong shell."

However, she joined in with gusto in the school's activities. She represented her house, Nightingale, at swimming and netball and developed her lifelong passion for dance. When

51

the annual nativity play came around she enjoyed the thrill of putting on makeup and dressing up. "I was one of those people who came and paid homage to Jesus," she recalls with amusement. At home she loved donning her sisters' clothes. An early picture shows her in a wide-brimmed black hat and white dress owned by Sarah.

While she respected Jane, the sensible member of the foursome, she hero-worshipped her eldest sister. When Sarah returned home from West Heath school, Diana was a willing servant, unpacking her suitcases, running her bath and tidying her room. Her loving domesticity was noticed not only by the Althorps' butler, Albert Betts, who recalls how she ironed her own jeans and performed other household duties, but also by her headmistress at Riddlesworth, Elizabeth Ridsdale — Riddy to pupils — who awarded her the Legatt Cup for helpfulness.

That achievement was greeted with satisfaction by her grandmother, Countess Spencer, who had kept an affectionate eye on Diana since the divorce. The feeling was mutual and when, in the autumn of 1972, she died of a brain tumour, Diana was heartbroken. She attended her memorial service along with the Queen Mother and Princess Margaret at the Chapel Royal in St James's Palace. Countess

Spencer holds a very special place in Diana's heart. She sincerely believes that her grandmother looks after her in the spirit world.

These otherworldly concerns gave way to more earthly considerations when Diana took the Common Entrance exam to enable her to follow in the footsteps of her sisters, Sarah and Jane, at West Heath boarding school set in 32 acres of parkland and woods outside Sevenoaks in Kent. The school, founded in 1865 on religious lines, emphasized the value of "character and confidence" as much as academic ability. Her sister Sarah had, however, shown a touch too much character for the liking of the headmistress, Ruth Rudge.

A competitor *par excellence*, Sarah passed six "O" levels, rode for the school team at Hickstead, starred in amateur dramatic productions and swam for the school team. Her strong competitive streak also meant that she had to be the most outrageous, the most rebellious and the most indisciplined girl in school. "She had to be the best at everything," recalls a contemporary. While her grandmother, Ruth, Lady Fermoy, forgave her when the exuberant redhead rode her horse into Park House when she was visiting, Miss Rudge could not excuse other instances of her colourful behaviour. Sarah complained that she was "bored", Miss Rudge told her to pack her bags and leave.

Jane, who captained the school lacrosse team, was a complete contrast to Sarah. Highly intelligent — she gained a hatful of "O" and "A" levels; eminently sensible and dependable, she was a prefect in the sixth form when Diana arrived.

Doubtless there was discussion in the teachers' common room about which sister the latest Spencer recruit to Poplar class would emulate, Sarah or Jane. It was a close run thing. Diana was in awe of her eldest sister but it wasn't until later in life that she forged a close relationship with Jane. During their youth Jane was more likely to put her weight and invective behind brother Charles than her kid sister. Diana's inevitable inclination was to imitate Sarah. During her first weeks she was noisy and disruptive in class. In an attempt to copy her sister Sarah's exploits she accepted a challenge which nearly got her expelled.

One evening her friends, reviewing the dwindling stocks of sweets in their tuck boxes, asked Diana to rendezvous with another girl at the end of the school drive and collect more supplies from her. It was a dare she accepted. As she walked down the treelined road in the pitch black she managed to suppress her fear of the dark. When she reached the school gate she discovered that there was no-one there.

She waited. And she waited. When two police cars raced in through the school gates she hid behind a wall.

Then she noticed the lights going on all over the school but thought no more about it. Finally she returned to her dorm, terrified not so much at the prospect of getting caught but because she had come back empty handed. As luck would have it a fellow pupil in Diana's dormitory complained that she had appendicitis. As she was being examined, Diana's teacher noticed the empty bed. The game was up. It was not just Diana who had to face the music but her parents as well. They were summoned to see Miss Rudge who took a dim view of the episode. Secretly Diana's parents were amused that their dutiful but docile daughter had displayed such spirit. "I didn't know you had it in you," said her mother afterwards.

While the incident curbed her wilder high jinks, Diana was always game for a dare. Food was a favourite challenge. "It was always a great joke: let's get Diana to eat three kippers and six slices of bread for breakfast," says one schoolfriend. "And she did." Her reputation as a glutton meant that while she often visited the matron with digestive problems these escapades did little harm to her popularity. On one birthday her friends clubbed together to buy her a necklace decorated with a "D" for Diana. Carolyn Pride, now Carolyn Bartholomew, who had the next bed in Diana's dormitory and later shared her London flat, remembers her as a "strong character, buoyant and noisy".

She added: "Jane was very popular, nice, unassuming but uncontroversial. Diana, by contrast, was much more full of life, a bubbly character." Carolyn and Diana were drawn to each other from the start because they were among the only pupils whose parents were divorced. "It wasn't a great trial to us and we didn't sit sobbing in a corner about it," she says although other pupils remember Diana as a "private and controlled" teenager who did not wear her emotions on her sleeve. It was noticeable that the two pictures which took pride of place on Diana's bedside dressing-table were not of her family but of her favourite hamsters, Little Black Muff and Little Black Puff.

However, she did fret constantly about her average academic abilities. Her sisters proved to be a hard act to follow while her brother, then at Maidwell Hall in Northamptonshire, was displaying the scholastic skills which later won him a place at Oxford University. The gawky teenager, who tended to stoop to disguise her height, longed to be as good as her

56

brother in the classroom. She was jealous and saw herself as a failure. "I wasn't any good at anything. I felt hopeless, a dropout," she says.

While she muddled through at maths and science she was more at home with subjects involving people. History, particularly the Tudors and Stuarts, fascinated her while in English she loved books like *Pride and Prejudice* and *Far from the Madding Crowd*. That didn't stop her from reading slushy romantic fiction by Barbara Cartland, soon to be her step-grandmother. In essays she wrote endlessly, her distinctive, well-rounded hand covering the pages. "It just came out of the pen, on and on and on," she says. Yet when it came to the silence of the examination hall, Diana froze. The five "O" levels she took in English literature and language, history, geography and art resulted in "D" grades which are fails.

The success which eluded her in the classroom did arrive but from an unexpected quarter. West Heath encouraged "good citizenship" by the girls, these ideas expressed in visits to the old, the sick and the mentally handicapped. Every week Diana and another girl saw an old lady in Sevenoaks. They chatted to her over tea and biscuits, tidied her house and did the odd spot of shopping. At the same time the local Voluntary Service Unit organized trips to Darenth Park, a large mental hospital near Dartford. Dozens of teenage volunteers were bussed in on Tuesday evening for a dance with mentally and physically handicapped patients.

Other youngsters helped with hyperactive teenagers who were so severely disturbed that to encourage a patient to smile was a major success story. "That's where she learned to go down on her hands and knees to meet people because most of the interaction was crawling with the patients," says Muriel Stevens who helped organize the visits. Many new school volunteers were apprehensive about visiting the hospital, anxieties fed by their fear of the unknown. However, Diana discovered that she had a natural aptitude for this work. She formed an instinctive rapport with many patients, her efforts giving her a real sense of achievement. It worked wonders for her sense of self-esteem.

At the same time she was a good all-round athlete. She won swimming and diving cups four years running. Her "Spencer Special", where she dived into the pool leaving barely a ripple, always attracted an audience. She was netball captain and played a creditable game of tennis. But she lived in the shadow of her sporty sisters and her mother who was "captain of everything" when she was at school and would have played at Junior Wimbledon but for an attack of appendicitis.

When Diana started to learn piano, any progress she made was always dwarfed by the achievements of her grandmother, Ruth, Lady Fermoy, who had performed at the Royal Albert Hall in front of the Queen Mother, and her sister Sarah who studied piano at a *conservatoire* in Vienna following her abrupt departure from West Heath. By contrast her community work was something she had achieved on her own without looking over her shoulder at the rest of her family. It was a satisfying first.

Dance gave her a further chance to shine. She loved her ballet and tap dancing sessions and longed to be a ballet dancer but, at 5ft 10½ inches, was too tall. A favourite ballet was *Swan Lake* which she saw at least four times when school parties travelled to the Coliseum or Sadler's Wells theatres in London. As she danced she could lose herself in the movement. Often she crept out of her bed in the dead of night and sneaked into the new school hall to practise. With music from a record player providing the background, Diana practised ballet for hours on end. "It always released tremendous tension in my head," she says. This extra effort paid dividends when she won the school dancing competition at the end of the spring term in 1976. Little wonder then that during the build-up to her wedding she invited her former teacher Wendy Mitchell and pianist Lily Snipp to Buckingham Palace so that she could have dancing lessons. For Diana it was an hour away from the stresses and strains of her new-found position.

When the family moved to Althorp in 1975 she had the perfect auditorium. On summer days she would practise her arabesques on the sandstone balustrades of the house and when the visitors had gone she danced in the black-and-white marble entrance hall, known officially as Wootton Hall, beneath portraits of her ancestors. They were not her only audience. While she refused to dance in public, her brother and staff took turns to look through the keyhole and watch her as she worked-out in her black leotard. "We were all very impressed," he says.

The family moved to Althorp following the death of her grandfather, the 7th Earl Spencer, on June 9, 1975. Although 83 he was still sprightly and his death from pneumonia following a short hospital stay came as a shock. It meant considerable upheaval. The girls all became Ladies, Charles, then aged eleven, was made a Viscount while their father became the 8th Earl and inherited Althorp. With 13,000 acres of rolling Northamptonshire farmland, more than 100 tied cottages, a valuable collection of paintings, several by Sir Joshua Reynolds, rare books, and seventeenth-century porcelain, furniture and silver, including the Marlborough collection, Althorp was not so much a stately home, more a way of life.

The new Earl also inherited a £2.25 million ($3.8 million) bill for death duties as well as £80,000 ($136,000) a year running costs. This did not prevent him paying for the installation of a swimming pool to amuse his children who roamed around their new domain during the holidays. Diana spent her days swimming, walking around the grounds, driving in Charles's blue beach buggy and, of course, dancing. The staff adored her, they found her friendly and unassuming with something of a passion for chocolates, sweets and the sugary romances of Barbara Cartland.

She eagerly awaited the days when Sarah arrived from London bringing with her a crowd of her sophisticated friends. Witty, and sharp, Sarah was seen by her contemporaries as the queen of the season especially after her father had organized a splendid coming-of-age party in 1973 at Castle Rising, a Norman castle in Norfolk. Guests arrived by horse-drawn carriages and the path to the Castle was lit by blazing torches. The lavish party is still talked about today. Her escorts matched her status. Everyone expected her relationship with Gerald Grosvenor, the Duke of Westminster and Britain's wealthiest aristocrat, to end in marriage. She was as surprised as anyone when he looked elsewhere.

Diana was happy to bask in her sister's glory. Lucinda Craig Harvey, who shared a house in London with Sarah and later employed Diana as a cleaner for £1 ($1.70) an hour, first met her prospective charlady during a cricket match at Althorp. First impressions were not flattering. Diana struck her as "a rather large girl who wore terrifying Laura Ashley maternity dresses". She says: "She was very shy, blushed easily and was very much the younger sister. Terribly unsophisticated, she certainly wasn't anything to look at." Nonetheless, Diana joined in the parties, the barbecues and the regular cricket matches with enthusiasm. These sporting contests between the house and the village ended with the arrival of a character who could have been dreamt up by central casting.

As a cryptic entry in the visitors' book noted: "Raine stopped play." Raine Spencer is not so much a person but a phenomenon. With her bouffant hairdo, elaborate plumage, gushing charm and bright smile she is a caricature of a countess. The daughter of the outspoken romantic novelist Barbara Cartland, she already had a half page entry in *Who's Who* before she met Johnnie Spencer. As Lady Lewisham and later after 1962 as the Countess of Dartmouth, she was a controversial figure in London politics where she served as a London County Councillor. Her colourful opinions soon gave her a wider platform and she became a familiar face in the gossip columns.

During the 1960s she became notorious as a parody of the "pearls and twinset" Tory councillor with views as rigid as her hairdos. "I always know when I visit Conservative houses because they wash their milk bottles before they put them out," was one howler which contributed to her being booed off the stage when she addressed students at the London School of Economics.

However her outspoken opinions mask an iron determination matched by a formidable charm and sharp turn of phrase. She and Earl Spencer worked on a book for the Greater London Council called *What is Our Heritage?* and soon found they had much in common. Raine was then 46 and had been married to the Earl of Dartmouth for 28 years. They had four children, William, Rupert, Charlotte, and Henry. During their schooldays at Eton, Johnnie Spencer and the Earl of Dartmouth had been good friends.

Raine wielded her overwhelming charm on

both father and son, effecting something of a reconciliation between Earl Spencer and her lover during the Earl's final years. The old Earl adored her, especially as for every birthday and Christmas she bought him a walking stick to add to his collection.

The children were less impressed. Like a galleon in full sail, she first hove into view during the early 1970s. Indeed her presence at Sarah's 18th birthday party at Castle Rising was the source of much muttering among the Norfolk gentry. A "sticky" dinner at the Duke's Head hotel in King's Lynn was the first real opportunity Charles and Diana had of assessing the new woman in their father's life. Ostensibly the dinner was organized to celebrate a tax plan which would save the family fortune. In reality it was a chance for Charles and Diana to get to know their prospective stepmother. "We didn't like her one bit," says Charles. They told their father that if he did marry her they would wash their hands of them. In 1976 Charles, then 12, spelled out his feelings by sending Raine a "vile" letter while Diana encouraged a schoolfriend to write her prospective stepmother a poison pen letter. The incident which prompted their behaviour was the discovery, shortly before the death of Diana's grandfather, of a letter which Raine had sent

to their father discu[...]
thorp. Her private opi[...]
Earl did not match the [...]
saw her behave in publi[...]
father.

With the family adaman[...]
match, Raine and Johnnie [...]
Caxton Hall register office [...]
shortly after he had been na[...]
proceedings by the Earl of Da[...]
of the children were told abou[...]
in advance and the first Charles[...]
new stepmother was when the he[...]
his prep school informed him.

Immediately a whirlwind of chan[...]
through Althorp as the new mistress[...]
oured to turn the family home into a[...]
proposition so that the awesome debts t[...]
Earl had taken on could be paid off. The[...]
were pared to the bone and in order to [...]
the house to paying visitors the stable bl[...]
was turned into a tea room and gift shop. Ov[...]
the years numerous paintings, antiques an[...]
other *objets d'art* have been sold often, claim[...]
the children, at rock bottom prices while they
describe in disdainful terms the way the house
has been "restored". Earl Spencer always
stoutly defended his wife's robust management of the estate saying: "The cost of res-
toration has been immense."

er there is no disguising the sour re-
at exist between Raine and his chil-
e publicly commented on the rift
e spoke to newspaper columnist Jean
"I'm absolutely sick of the 'Wicked
ther' lark. You're never going to make
nd like a human being, because people
think I'm Dracula's mother but I did
a rotten time at the start and it's only
getting better. Sarah resented me, even
place at the head of the table, and gave
rs to the servants over my head. Jane
n't speak to me for two years, even if we
mped in a passageway. Diana was sweet,
ways did her own thing."

In fact, Diana's indignation at Raine sim-
ered for years until finally it boiled over in
989 at the church rehearsal for her brother's
wedding to Victoria Lockwood, a successful
model. Raine refused to speak to Diana's
mother in church even though they were
seated together in the same pew. Diana vented
all the grievances which had been welling up
inside her for more than ten years. As Diana
challenged her Raine replied: "You have no
idea how much pain your mother put your
father through." Diana, who has since admitted that she had never felt such fury, rounded
on her stepmother. "Pain Raine. That's one
word you don't even know how to relate to.

In my role I see people suffer like you'll never see and you call that pain. You've got a lot to learn." There was much more in the same vein. Afterwards her mother said that was the first time anyone in the family had defended her.

However in the early days of her tenure at Althorp, the children simply treated Raine as a joke. They played upon her penchant for pigeonholing house guests into their appropriate social categories. When Charles arrived from Eton, where he was then at school, he had primed his friends beforehand to give false names. So one boy said that he was "James Rothschild", implying that he was a member of the famous banking family. Raine brightened. "Oh, are you Hannah's son?", she asked. Charles's schoolfriend said that he didn't know before compounding his folly by spelling the surname incorrectly in the visitors' book.

At a weekend barbecue one of Sarah's friends wagered £100 that Charles couldn't throw his stepmother into the swimming pool. Raine, who appeared at this shorts and T-shirts party in a ballgown, agreed to Charles's request for a dance by the pool. As he tensed for a judo throw, she realized what was going on and slipped away. Christmas at Althorp with Raine Spencer in charge was a bizarre comedy, a sharp contrast to the extravagances of Park House. She presided over the present-opening like an officious timekeeper. The children were only allowed to open the present she indicated and only after she had looked at her watch to give the go-ahead to tear the paper off. "It was completely mad," says Charles.

The only bright spot was when Diana decided to give one of her presents away to a rather irascible nightwatchman. While he had a fearsome reputation, Diana instinctively felt that he was just lonely. She and her brother went to see him and he was so touched by her gesture that he burst into tears. It was an early example of her sensitivity to the needs of others, a quality noticed by her headmistress, Miss Rudge, who awarded her the Miss Clark Lawrence Award for service to the school in her last term in 1977.

Diana was now growing in self-confidence, a quality recognized by her elevation to school prefect. When she left West Heath, Diana followed in sister Sarah's footsteps by enrolling at the Institut Alpin Videmanette, an expensive finishing school near Gstaad in Switzerland, where Diana took classes in domestic science, dressmaking and cookery. She was supposed to speak nothing but French all day. In fact she and her friend Sophie Kimball spoke English all the time and the only thing she cultivated was her skiing. Unhappy and stifled by school routine, Diana was desperate to escape. She wrote scores of letters pleading with her parents to bring her home. Finally they relented when she argued that they were simply wasting their money.

With her schooldays behind her, Diana felt as if some great weight had been lifted from her shoulders. She visibly blossomed, becoming jollier, livelier and prettier. Diana was now more mature and relaxed and her sisters' friends looked at her with new eyes. Still shy and overweight, she was nevertheless developing into a popular character. "She was great fun, charming and kind," says a friend.

However, the blooming of Diana was viewed with jealous misgivings by Sarah. London was her kingdom and she didn't want her sister taking the spotlight away from her. The crunch came on one of the last of the old-style weekends at Althorp. Diana asked her sister for a lift to London. Sarah refused saying that it would cost too much in petrol to have an extra person in the car. Her friends ridiculed her, seeing for the first time how the balance in their relationship had shifted in favour of adorable Diana.

Diana had been the Cinderella of her family for long enough. She had felt her spirit suppressed by school routine and her character cramped by her minor position in the family. Diana was eager to spread her wings and start her own life in London. The thrill of independence beckoned. As her brother Charles says: "Suddenly the insignificant ugly duckling was obviously going to be a swan."

3

"Just Call Me 'Sir'"

By any standards it was an unusual romance. It was not until Lady Diana Spencer was formally engaged to His Royal Highness the Prince of Wales that she was given permission to call him "Charles". Until then she had demurely addressed him as "Sir". He called her Diana. In Prince Charles's circle this was considered the norm. When Diana's sister Sarah enjoyed a nine-month long relationship with the Prince of Wales she had been as formal. "It just seemed natural," she recalls. "It was obviously right to do so because I was never corrected."

It was during her sister's romance that Diana first came into the path of the man considered then to be the world's most eligible bachelor. That historic meeting in November 1977 was hardly auspicious. Diana, on weekend leave from West Heath school, was introduced to the Prince in the middle of a ploughed field near Nobottle Wood on the Althorp estate during a day's shooting. The Prince, who brought along his faithful labrador, Sandringham Harvey, is considered to be one of the finest shots in the country so he was more intent on sport than small talk on that bleak afternoon. Diana cut a nondescript figure in her checked shirt, her sister's anorak, cords and wellington boots. She kept in the background, realizing that she had only been brought along to make up numbers. It was very much her sister's show and Sarah was perhaps being rather mischievous when she said later that she "played Cupid" between her kid sister and the Prince.

If Charles's first memories of Diana on that fateful weekend are of "a very jolly and amusing and attractive 16-year-old — full of fun", then it was certainly no thanks to her elder sister. As far as Sarah was concerned Charles was her domain at that time and trespassers were not welcome by the sparky redhead who applied her competitive instincts to the men in her life. In any case Diana was not overly impressed by Sarah's royal boyfriend. "What a sad man," she remembers thinking. The Spencers held a dance that weekend in his honour and it was noticeable that Sarah was enthusiastic in her attentions. Diana has since told friends: "I kept out of the way. I remember being podgy, no make-up, an unsmart lady but I made a lot of noise and he seemed to like that."

When dinner was over he liked Diana enough to ask her to show him the 115-foot-long picture gallery which then housed one of the finest private collections of art in Europe. Sarah wanted to be the guide to the family's "etchings". Diana took the hint and left them to it.

While Sarah's behaviour was hardly that of a would-be Cupid, Charles's interest in her younger sister left Diana with much food for thought. He was, after all, her sister's boyfriend. Charles and Sarah had met at Ascot in June 1977 when Sarah was licking her wounds after her romance with the Duke of Westminster had ended. At that time she was suffering from anorexia nervosa, a slimming disease, which friends believe was triggered by the collapse of her love affair. As one friend notes: "Sarah always had to be the best at everything. The best car, the wittiest put-down, and the best dress. Dieting was part of her competitive nature, to be thinner than everybody else."

While that incident may have precipitated the disease, eating disorder experts observe that the illness is seated in family life. The majority of sufferers are teenage girls with strong characters who come from disturbed family backgrounds. They see food as a way of controlling both their bodies and the chaos they feel about their lives. Anorexics, who will use all manner of subterfuge to avoid eating, often become so thin that they lose their monthly periods and consequently have difficulty becoming pregnant. Four out of ten die.

Sarah has kept a picture of herself in her underwear when she was literally skin and bone. At that time, during the mid-1970s, she thought she was fat. Now she realizes how sick she was. Her family, worried about her health, used every method possible to encourage her to eat. For example she would be allowed to speak to Prince Charles on the telephone if she put on two pounds. In 1977 she elected to go to a nursing home in Regent's Park where she was treated by Dr Maurice Lipsedge, a psychiatrist who, by pure coincidence, cared for Diana a decade later when she resolved to fight her bulimia.

As she tried to overcome her illness, Sarah frequently saw Prince Charles. During the summer of 1977 she watched him play polo at Smith's Lawn, Windsor and when, in February 1978, he invited her to join him on a skiing party in Klosters, Switzerland there was much speculation that she might be the future queen of England. However Sarah's enjoyment of publicity overcame the circumspection a royal girlfriend is expected to display.

She gave a magazine interview which considerably dented Prince Charles's image as a charming Casanova. "Our relationship is totally platonic," she stated. "I think of him as the big brother I never had." For good measure she added: "I wouldn't marry a man I didn't love, whether it was a dustman or the King of England. If he asked me I would turn him down."

While their romance cooled-off, Charles still asked Sarah to attend his 30th birthday party at Buckingham Palace in November 1978. Much to Sarah's surprise, Diana was also invited. Cinderella was going to the ball.

Diana enjoyed herself enormously at the birthday party not least because it brought her sister down a peg or two. Yet it never entered her head for a moment to think that Prince Charles was remotely interested in romance. Certainly she never considered herself a match for the actress Susan George, who was his escort that evening. In any case, life was much too enjoyable to think about steady boyfriends. She had returned from her excursion to the Swiss finishing school desperate to begin an independent life in London. Her parents were not enthusiastic.

She had no paper qualifications, no special skills and only a vague notion that she wanted to work with children. While Diana seemed destined for a life of unskilled, low-paying jobs, she was not that much out of the ordinary for girls of her class and background. Aristocratic families traditionally invest more thought and effort in educating boys than girls. There is a tacit assumption that, after rounding off their formal education with a cookery or arts course, daughters will join their well-bred friends on the marriage market. At the start of the Queen's reign this feature of the London season was still formalized in the presentation of debutantes at Buckingham Palace which was followed by a series of coming-out balls. Indeed Diana's parents had met at her mother's coming-out ball in April 1953, while in her day Raine, Countess Spencer was voted "Deb of the Year".

Marriage was very much in Diana's mind when she returned from Switzerland. Her sister Jane had asked her to be chief bridesmaid at her wedding to Robert Fellowes, the son of the Queen's land agent at Sandringham and now her private secretary, which was held in the Guards Chapel in April 1978. While there was no pressure from her family to embark on a structured career, there was considerable reluctance about allowing her to live on her own in London. As her Swiss headmistress Madame Yersin commented: "She was rather young for a sixteen-year-old." If she was an innocent abroad, her parents considered that a life cocooned in an all-girls school was hardly adequate preparation for the bright lights of the big city. They told her that she couldn't have her own flat until she was eighteen.

Instead she was farmed out to family friends, Major Jeremy Whitaker, a photographer, and his wife Philippa who lived in Headley Bawden in Hampshire. She stayed with them for three months and as well as looking after their daughter Alexandra she cleaned and cooked. Yet she was itching to move to the metropolis and bombarded her parents with subtle and not so subtle requests. Finally a compromise was reached. Her mother allowed her to stay at her flat in Cadogan Square. As Mrs Shand Kydd spent most of the year in Scotland it was as good as her own place. It was to be her home for a year, sharing it initially with Laura Greig, an old schoolchum and now one of her ladies-in-waiting, and Sophie Kimball, the daughter of the then Conservative Member of Parliament, Marcus Kimball.

In order to earn her keep Diana joined the ranks of what she now dismissively refers to as the "velvet hairband" brigade, the upper-class ladies who fit a loose template of values, fashions, breeding and attitudes and are commonly known as "Sloane Rangers". She signed up for two employment agencies: Solve Your Problems and Knightsbridge Nannies, and worked as a waitress at private parties and as a charlady. In between driving lessons — she passed her test at the second attempt — she was much in demand as a babysitter by her sisters' married friends while Sarah used her to make up numbers at her frequent dinner parties. Her London life was sedate, almost mundane. She didn't smoke and never drank, preferring to spend her free time reading, watching television, visiting friends or going out for supper in modest bistros. Noisy nightclubs, wild parties or smoky pubs were never her scene. "Disco Di" has only ever existed in the minds of headline writers with an appreciation for alliteration. In reality Diana is a loner by inclination and habit.

Weekends were spent in the country, at Althorp with her father, at her sister Jane's cottage on the estate or at a house party organized by one of her growing circle of friends. Her friends from Norfolk and West Heath, Alexandra Loyd, Caroline Harbord-Hammond, the daughter of Lord Suffield, Theresa Mowbray, the goddaughter of Frances Shand Kydd, and Mary-Ann Stewart-Richardson, were all now living in London and formed the nucleus of her set.

It was while she was staying with Caroline

one weekend in September 1978 at her parents' Norfolk home that she had a disturbing premonition. When she was politely asked about her father's health her reply startled the assembled company. She found herself saying that she felt her father was going to "drop down" in some way. "If he dies, he will die immediately otherwise he will survive," she said. The following day the telephone rang. Diana knew it was about her father. It was. Earl Spencer had collapsed in the courtyard at Althorp suffering from a massive cerebral haemorrhage and had been rushed to Northampton General Hospital. Diana packed her bags and joined her sisters and brother Charles who had been driven from Eton by his brother-in-law, Robert Fellowes.

The medical prognosis was bleak. Earl Spencer was not expected to survive the night. According to his son, Charles, Raine Spencer was matter of fact. He remembers her telling his brother-in-law: "I'll be out of Althorp first thing in the morning." The reign of Raine seemed to be over. For two days the children camped out in the hospital waiting-room as their father clung on to life. When doctors announced that there was a glimmer of hope, Raine organized a private ambulance to take him to the National Hospital for Nervous Diseases in Queen Square, central London where for several months he lay in a coma. As the family kept vigil, the children saw at close quarters the stubborn determination of their stepmother. She tried to stop the children visiting their critically ill father. Nurses were instructed to prevent them from seeing Earl Spencer as he lay helpless in his private room. As Raine has said since: "I'm a survivor and people forget that at their peril. There's pure steel up my backbone. Nobody destroys me, and nobody was going to destroy Johnnie so long as I could sit by his bed — some of his family tried to stop me — and will my life force into him."

During this critical time the ill feeling between Raine and the children boiled over into a series of vicious exchanges. There was iron too in the Spencer soul and numerous hospital corridors rang to the sound of the redoubtable Countess and the fiery Lady Sarah Spencer hissing at each other like a pair of angry geese.

In November Earl Spencer suffered a relapse and was moved to the Brompton Hospital in South Kensington. Once again his life hung in the balance. When his doctors were at their most pessimistic, Raine's will-power won through. She had heard of a German drug called Aslocillin which she thought could help and so she pulled every string to find a supply. It was unlicensed in Britain but that didn't stop her. The wonder drug was duly acquired and miraculously did the trick. One afternoon she was maintaining her usual bedside vigil when, with the strains of *Madam Butterfly* playing in the background, he opened his eyes "and was back". In January 1979 when he was finally released from hospital he and Raine booked into the Dorchester Hotel in Park Lane for an expensive month-long convalescence.

Throughout this episode the strain on the family was intense. Sarah, who lived near to the Brompton Hospital, visited her father regularly although Raine's hostility complicated an already fraught situation. When she was absent sympathetic nurses allowed Diana and Jane to see him but with Earl Spencer drifting in and out of consciousness he was never aware of the presence of his children. Even when he was awake a feeding tube in his throat meant that he was unable to speak. As Diana has recalled: "He wasn't able to ask where his children were. Goodness knows what he was thinking because no-one was telling him."

Understandably Diana found it hard to concentrate on the cookery course she had enrolled in a few days before her father suffered his stroke. For three months she went by Underground to the Wimbledon home of Elizabeth Russell where for almost as long as anyone can remember she has schooled the daughters of knights, dukes and earls in the delights of sauces, sponges and soufflés. As far as Diana was concerned it was another set of "velvet hairbands". She had joined the course at her parents' insistence and while it wasn't her idea of fun at the time it seemed a better alternative than being behind a typewriter. Often the glutton in Diana got the better of her and she was frequently told off for dipping her fingers into pans filled with gooey sauces. She completed the course a few pounds heavier and clutching a diploma for her efforts.

As her father began his fight back to health, Diana's mother took a hand in guiding her career. She wrote to Miss Betty Vacani, the legendary dance teacher who has taught three generations of royal children, and asked if there was a vacancy for a student ballet teacher at grade two level. There was. Diana passed her interview and, in the spring term, began at the Vacani dance studio on the Brompton Road. It neatly combined her love of children with her enjoyment of dance. Again she only lasted three months but for once it wasn't her fault.

In March her friend Mary-Ann Stewart-Richardson invited her to join her family on their skiing holiday in the French Alps. Diana fell badly on the ski slopes, tearing all the tendons in her left ankle. For three months she was in and out of plaster as the tendons slowly heeled. It marked the end of her aspirations as a dance teacher.

In spite of her misadventure, Diana looks back on that trip to Val Claret as one of the most enjoyable and carefree holidays of her life. It is also where she first met many of the people who have since become loyal and supportive friends. When Diana joined the Stewart-Richardsons they were just coming to terms with a family tragedy. She naturally felt out of place in their chalet and accepted the invitation of Simon Berry, the son of a wealthy wine merchant, to join his chalet party.

Berry and three other old Etonians, James Bolton, Alex Lyle and Christian De Lotbiniere, were the brains behind "Ski Bob" travel. This was a company, named after their Eton housemaster Bob Baird, which had been formed when they discovered that they were too young legally to book holidays themselves. So these young entrepreneurs started their own company and within the twenty-strong group, which mainly compromised old Etonians, the greatest accolade was to be called "Bob".

Diana was soon Bob, Bob, Bobbing along. "You're skating on thin ice," she yelled in her Miss Piggy voice as she skiied dangerously close behind members of the group. She joined in the pillow fights, charades and satirical sing-songs. Diana was teased mercilessly about a framed photograph of Prince Charles, taken at his Investiture in 1969, which hung in her school dormitory. Not guilty, she said. It was a gift to the school. When she stayed in the Berry chalet she slept on the living-room sofa. Not that she got much sleep. Medical student, James Colthurst, liked to regale the slumbering throng with unwelcome early morning renditions of Martin Luther King's famous "I had a dream" speech or his equally unamusing Mussolini impersonation.

Adam Russell, the great-grandson of former Prime Minister Stanley Baldwin and now a deer farmer in Dorset, was not overly impressed by Diana when she first walked in. He recalls: "When she arrived she made a rude comment followed by a giggle. I thought: 'Oh God, a giggler, help.' Once you got behind that she was very much more composed. But she was lacking in self-confidence when she should have had lots. Very bubbly and giggly but not in a vacuous way." When he too was injured, they kept each other company and during their conversations he saw the reflective, rather sad side to her character. He says: "She seemed a happy person on the surface but underneath she had been deeply affected by her parents' divorce."

Her sister Sarah, then working for Savills, a leading estate agent, found what was to become, for a time, the most famous address in Britain. A three-bedroomed apartment in a mansion block at 60, Coleherne Court was Diana's coming-of-age present from her parents. In July 1979 she moved into the £50,000 ($85,000) apartment and immediately set to work furnishing the rooms in a warm but simple Habitat style. The white walls were repainted in pastel shades, the sitting room became pale primrose yellow while the bathroom was bright with red cherries. Diana had always promised her schoolfriend, Carolyn Bartholomew, a room when she got her own apartment. She was as good as her word. Sophie Kimball and Philippa Coaker stayed for a while but in August Diana and Carolyn were joined by Anne Bolton, who also worked for Savills, and Virginia Pitman, the oldest member of the quartet. It was these three who stayed with her throughout her romance with Prince Charles.

Diana now looks back on those days at Coleherne Court as the happiest time of her life. It was juvenile, innocent, uncomplicated and above all fun. "I laughed my head off there," she says and the only black cloud was when the apartment was burgled and she had most of her jewellery stolen. As landlady, she charged the others £18 ($31) a week and organized the cleaning rotas. Naturally she had the largest room, complete with double bed. So that no-one would forget her status, the words "Chief Chick" were emblazoned on her bedroom door. "She always had the rubber gloves on as she clucked about the place," recalls Carolyn. "But it was her house and when it is your own you are incredibly proud of it."

At least she never had to worry about washing piles of dirty dishes and cups. The girls rarely cooked in spite of the fact that Virginia and Diana had completed expensive *cordon bleu* courses. Diana's two specialities were chocolate roulades and Russian borscht soup which friends asked her to make and then deliver to their apartments. Usually the girls devoured the roulade before it left Coleherne Court. Otherwise they lived on Harvest Crunch bran cereal and chocolate. "We stayed remarkably plump," observes Carolyn.

The houseproud teenager was also tidying up her career. Shortly after moving into her apartment she found a job where she was truly in her element. For several afternoons a week she went to work at the Young England kindergarten run by Victoria Wilson and Kay Seth-Smith in St Saviour's church hall in

Pimlico. She taught the children painting, drawing and dancing and joined in the games they devised. Victoria and Kay were so impressed with her rapport with the children that they asked her to work in the morning as well. On Tuesdays and Thursdays she looked after Patrick Robinson, the son of an American oil executive, work which she "adored".

There were still loose ends in her working week so her sister Sarah took it upon herself to tie them up. She employed her as a cleaner at her house in Elm Park Lane, Chelsea. Sarah's flatmate Lucinda Craig Harvey recalls: "Diana hero-worshipped her but Sarah treated her like a doormat. She told me not to be embarrassed about asking Diana to do the washing up and so on." Diana, who did the vacuuming, dusting, ironing and washing, was paid £1 ($1.70) an hour and took a quiet satisfaction in her labours. When she became engaged to Prince Charles Diana referred to her cleaning job in her reply to Lucinda's letter of congratulation. "Gone are the days of Jif and dusters. Oh dear will I ever see them again?"

She escaped her sister's gimlet gaze when she returned to the privacy of her own apartment. Perhaps this was just as well since the jolly but rather juvenile japes her sister embarked upon might not have pleased her.

Diana and Carolyn would regularly while away a quiet evening ringing people with silly names who appeared in the telephone directory. Another favourite pastime was planning raids on the various apartments and cars owned by their friends. Carolyn recalls: "We used to do midnight runs, we were always skimming around London on undercover operations in Diana's Metro."

Those who offended the girls in some way were paid back with interest. Doorbells were rung in the dead of night, early morning alarm calls were made, friends' cars had their locks covered in sticky tape. On one occasion James Gilbey, then working for a car rental company in Victoria, woke to find his prize Alfa Romeo car covered in eggs and flour which had set like concrete. For some reason he had let down Diana on a date so she and Carolyn had taken their revenge.

It wasn't all one way traffic. One evening James Colthurst and Adam Russell secretly tied two huge "L" plates to the front and rear of Diana's Honda Civic car. She managed to pull them off but as she drove down the street she was followed by a cacophony of tin cans tied to the bumper. Once again eggs and flour were used by Diana and Carolyn in high-spirited retaliation.

Indeed this innocent, totally unsophisticated

fun continued throughout her romance with Prince Charles. "We were the giggling lavatorial girls we've always been portrayed but somewhere there was a spark of maturity," says Carolyn. Certainly the constant parade of young men calling round for a chat and tea, if there was any, or to take the girls out for the evening were friends who happened to be boys. For the most part Diana's escorts were old Etonians whom she had met while skiing or elsewhere. Harry Herbert, the son of the Queen's racing manager, the Earl of Carnarvon, James Boughey, a lieutenant in the Coldstream Guards, farmer's son George Plumptre, who asked her to the ballet the day she got engaged, the artist Marcus May and Rory Scott, then a dashing lieutenant in the Royal Scots Guards, often came to call, along with Simon Berry, Adam Russell, and James Colthurst. "We were all just friends together," Simon Berry remembers.

The men in her life were clean-cut, well-bred, reliable, unpretentious and good company. "Diana is an Uptown girl who has never gone in for downtown men," observes Rory Scott. If they wore a uniform or had been cast aside by Sarah so much the better. She felt rather sorry for Sarah's rejects and often tried, unsuccessfully, to be asked out by them.

So she did washing for William van

Straubenzee, one of Sarah's old boyfriends, and ironed the shirts of Rory Scott, who had then starred in a television documentary about Trooping the Colour, and Diana regularly stayed for weekends at his parents' farm near Petworth, West Sussex. She continued caring for his wardrobe during her royal romance, on one occasion delivering a pile of freshly laundered shirts to the back entrance of St James's Palace, where Rory was on duty, in order to avoid the press. James Boughey was another military man who took her out to restaurants and the theatre and Diana visited Simon Berry and Adam Russell at their rented house on the Blenheim estate when they were undergraduates at Oxford.

There were lots of boyfriends but none became lovers. The sense of destiny which Diana had felt from an early age shaped, albeit unconsciously, her relationships with the opposite sex. She says: "I knew I had to keep myself tidy for what lay ahead."

As Carolyn observes: "I'm not a terribly spiritual person but I do believe that she was meant to do what she is doing and she certainly believes that. She was surrounded by this golden aura which stopped men going any further, whether they would have liked to or not, it never happened. She was protected somehow by a perfect light."

It is a quality noted by her old boyfriends. Rory Scott says roguishly: "She was very sexually attractive and the relationship was not a platonic one as far as I was concerned but it remained that way. She was always a little aloof, you always felt that there was a lot you would never know about her."

In the summer of 1979 another boyfriend, Adam Russell, completed his language degree at Oxford and decided to spend a year travelling. He left unspoken the fact that he hoped the friendship between himself and Diana could be renewed and developed upon his return. When he arrived home a year later it was too late. A friend told him: "You've only got one rival, the Prince of Wales."

That winter Diana's star began to move into the royal family's orbit. She received an unexpected Christmas bonus in the form of an invitation to join a royal house party at Sandringham for a shooting weekend in February. Lucinda Craig Harvey, known to all her friends as Beryl, remembers Diana's excitement and the irony of the subsequent conversation. They were chatting about the weekend while Diana, ever the Cinderella, was on her knees cleaning the kitchen floor. Diana said: "Guess what, I'm going on a shooting weekend to Sandringham." Lucinda replied: "Gosh, perhaps you are going to be the next queen of England." As she wrung out a cloth which she was using to mop the floor Diana joked: "Beryl, I doubt it. Can you see me swanning around in kid gloves and a ball-gown?"

As Diana's life was taking a new direction, her sister Sarah was in crisis. She and Neil McCorquodale, a former Coldstream Guards officer, had abruptly called off their wedding which was planned for later in February. In true Spencer style — it is certainly not a family for the faint-hearted — there were angry words and exchanges of letters between the interested parties. While Sarah was trying to sort out the mess — they eventually married in May 1980 at St Mary's church near Althorp — Diana was having fun. For once Diana was in what she calls "a grown up" social setting. This for Diana was the satisfaction of that Sandringham weekend, not her proximity to Prince Charles. She was still in awe of the man, her sense of respect mellowed by a feeling of deep sympathy for the Prince whose "honorary grandfather", Earl Mountbatten, had been assassinated by the IRA just six months previously. In any case the following Monday as she scrubbed her sister's floors this aristocratic Cinderella had to pinch herself to make sure that her weekend was not some idle pipe-dream.

For whatever that small voice of intuition was telling her about her destiny, common-sense decreed that the Prince already had a full hand of potential suitors. She travelled to King's Lynn and then on to Sandringham with Lady Amanda Knatchbull, the granddaughter of the murdered Earl. Lord Mountbatten had strenuously pressed her suit not only on the Prince of Wales but the royal family. After all it was he, in the face of George VI's reservations, who was instrumental in clearing the decks for the union of Princess Elizabeth and Prince Philip.

While commentators have dismissed her as a serious contender, those who worked intimately with the Prince and watched Mountbatten's machinations at first-hand were convinced that marriage between Prince Charles and Amanda Knatchbull was a virtual certainty. A glance through his working diary for 1979 shows how frequently Prince Charles stayed at Broadlands, the Mountbatten family seat, ostensibly for fishing and shooting weekends. Amanda was a frequent companion and, according to those working for the Prince, it was only the discovery of her friendship with a diplomat which prevented the match going any further. In the aftermath of Mountbatten's murder in August 1979, Charles's friendship with Lady Amanda developed and he spent several weekends in her company as they tried to come to terms with their loss. If the unofficial "queenmaker" had lived and Lady Amanda's friendship remained undiscovered, royal history might have been very different.

While Amanda may be considered as the "official candidate" whose breeding and background made her eminently acceptable at Court, the Prince was also conducting a stormy relationship with Anna Wallace, the daughter of a Scottish landowner whom he had met while fox hunting in November 1979. She was the latest of a long line of girlfriends, drawn for the most part from the upper reaches of the aristocracy, who had appeared on his romantic horizon. However Anna, fiery, wilful and impulsive, was temperamentally unsuitable for the regulated routine of royalty. Not for nothing was she known as "Whiplash Wallace". Prince Charles, a man who by his own admission fell in love easily, pressed his suit even though his advisers told him that she had other boy-friends.

Their relationship became so serious that, according to at least one account, he asked her to marry him. She is said to have turned him down but that rebuff did little to dampen his ardour. In May they were discovered by journalists lying on a blanket by the river Dee on the Queen's estate at Balmoral. The Prince was furious at this intrusion into his private life and authorized his friend, Lord Tryon, who was present at the picnic to shout a four letter word at the journalists concerned.

The end of their romance in the middle of June was just as tempestuous. She complained bitterly when he virtually ignored her during a ball to celebrate the Queen Mother's 80th birthday at Windsor Castle. Anna was overheard to rage: "Don't ignore me like that again. I've never been treated so badly in my life. No-one treats me like that, not even you." On their next public appearance he treated her in precisely the same way. She watched with mounting fury as he danced the night away with Camilla Parker-Bowles at a polo ball held at Stowell Park, the Gloucestershire estate owned by Lord Vestey. He was so eager for Camilla's company that he did not even ask his hostess, Lady Vestey, to take the floor. In the end, Anna borrowed Lady Vestey's BMW car and drove off into the night, angry and humiliated at her very public snub. Within a month she married Johnny Hesketh, the younger brother of Lord Hesketh.

With hindsight it is tempting to ask if her outrage was directed at the Prince or the woman who held him in such thrall, Camilla Parker-Bowles. If Prince Charles was serious about marrying Anna then she, a worldly wise

25-year-old, would have been aware of the nature of his friendship with Camilla. She would have known, as Diana discovered too late, that Camilla's famous vetting of Charles's girlfriends was not so much to assess their potential as a royal bride but to see how much of a threat they posed to her own relationship with Prince Charles. Perhaps Anna saw the unmistakable chemistry between Camilla and Charles and decided to leave the fray.

She might also have simply got tired of playing second fiddle to the Prince's pastimes. Throughout his bachelor years — and during his marriage — his partners have simply fitted in to his lifestyle. They were interested spectators while he played polo, went fishing or fox hunting. When he entertained them to dinner, they travelled to his apartment at Buckingham Palace, not the other way around. His staff organized boxes for concerts or the opera and even remembered to send flowers to his escorts. "A charming male chauvinist" is how one friend describes him. His behaviour, as the Victorian constitutionalist Walter Bagehot had noted a hundred years earlier, was the prerogative of princes. He wrote: "All the world and the glory of it, whatever is most attractive, whatever is most seductive, has always been offered to the Prince of Wales of the day, and always will be. It is not rational to expect the best virtue where temptation is applied in the most trying form at the frailest time of human life."

That summer of 1980 Prince Charles was a man of settled habits and inflexible routine. A former member of his Household, reviewing the collapse of the Waleses' marriage, sincerely believes that he would have remained single if he had been given the choice. He recalls: "It's very sad really. He would never have got married, of course, because he was happy with his bachelor life. If he had his fishing tackle ready, his polo ponies saddled and a £5 note for the church collection he was perfectly content. It was great fun. You would wake him up at six in the morning and say: 'Right Sir we are going here' and off we would go." His friendship with Camilla Parker-Bowles, who eagerly adapted her life to his diary, dovetailed perfectly with his lifestyle.

Unfortunately for Charles, his title brought obligations as well as privileges. His duty was to marry and produce an heir to the throne. It was a subject Earl Mountbatten discussed endlessly with the Queen during afternoon tea at Buckingham Palace while Prince Philip let it be known that he was growing impatient with his son's irresponsible approach to marriage. The ghost of the Duke of Windsor haunted the minds of the family, patently aware that the older he became the more difficult it would be to find a virginal, Protestant aristocrat to be his bride.

His quest for a wife had developed into a national pastime. The Prince, then nearly 33, had already made himself a hostage to fortune by declaring that 30 was a suitable age to settle down. He publicly acknowledged the problems of finding a suitable bride. "Marriage is a much more important business than falling in love. I think one must concentrate on marriage being essentially a question of mutual love and respect for each other . . . Essentially you must be good friends, and love, I'm sure, will grow out of that friendship. I have a particular responsibility to ensure that I make the right decision. The last thing I could possibly entertain is getting divorced."

On another occasion he declared that marriage was a partnership where his wife was not simply marrying the man but a way of life. As he said: "If I'm deciding on whom I want to live with for fifty years — well, that's the last decision I want my head to be ruled by my heart." Thus marriage in his eyes was primarily the discharge of an obligation to his family and the nation, a task made all the more difficult by the immutable nature of the contract. In his pragmatic search for a partner to fulfill a role, love and happiness were secondary considerations.

The meeting which was to set Prince Charles and Lady Diana Spencer irrevocably on the road to St Paul's Cathedral took place in July 1980 on a hay bale at the home of Commander Robert de Pass, a friend of Prince Philip, and his wife Philippa, a lady-in-waiting to the Queen. Diana was invited to stay at their house in Petworth, West Sussex by their son Philip. "You're a young blood," he told her, "you might like him."

During the weekend she drove to nearby Cowdray Park to watch the Prince play polo for his team, Les Diables Bleus. At the end of the game the small house party trooped back to Petworth for a barbecue in the grounds of the de Passes' country home. Diana was seated next to Charles on a bale of hay and, after the usual pleasantries, the conversation moved on to Earl Mountbatten's death and his funeral in Westminster Abbey. In a conversation which she later recalled to friends Diana told him: "You looked so sad when you walked up the aisle at the funeral. It was the most tragic thing I've ever seen. My heart bled for you when I watched it. I thought: 'It's wrong, you are lonely, you should be with somebody to look after you.'"

Her words touched a deep chord. Charles saw Diana with new eyes. Suddenly, as she later told her friends, she found herself overwhelmed by his enthusiastic attentions. Diana was flattered, flustered and bewildered by the passion she had aroused in a man twelve years her senior. They resumed their conversation, chatting away late into the evening. The Prince, who had important paperwork to attend to at Buckingham Palace, asked her to drive back with him the following day. She refused on the grounds that it would be rude to her hosts.

However, from that point their relationship began to develop. Her flatmate, Carolyn Bartholomew, recalls: "Prince Charles was coming quietly on to the scene. She certainly had a special place for him in her heart." He invited her to a performance of Verdi's *Requiem* — one of her favourite works — at the Royal Albert Hall. Her grandmother, Ruth, Lady Fermoy, went along as their chaperone and accompanied them when they returned to Buckingham Palace for a cold buffet supper in his apartments. His memo to his valet, then the late Stephen Barry, relating to the meeting is typical of the elaborate planning undertaken for the simplest royal date. It read: "Please ring Captain Anthony Asquith [a former equerry] before going out shooting and tell him that I have asked Lady Diana Spencer (Lady Fermoy's granddaughter) to come to the Albert Hall and dinner afterwards at BP on Sunday evening. Please ask him if this can be arranged and she will arrive with her grandmother at the Albert Hall. If it is allright please ask him to ring back at lunchtime when we will be in the House. C." [The House is Buckingham Palace.]

The problem is that the invitation must have come rather late as Carolyn recalls: "I walked in about six o'clock and Diana went: 'Quick, quick I've got to meet Charles in twenty minutes.' Well, we had the funniest time ever, getting the hair washed, getting it dried, getting the dress, where's the dress. We did it in twenty minutes flat. But I mean, how dare he ask her so late."

She had scarcely recovered her composure from that frantic evening before he invited her to join him on the royal yacht *Britannia* during Cowes Week. The royal yacht, the oldest ship in the Royal Navy, is a familiar sight in the waters of the Solent during the August regatta and Prince Philip plays host to a party which usually includes his German relatives along with Princess Alexandra, her husband, Sir Angus Ogilvy and numerous yachting friends.

On that weekend Diana had Lady Sarah Armstrong-Jones, Princess Margaret's daughter, and Susan Deptford, who later became

Major Ronald Ferguson's second wife, to keep her company. She went water skiing while Prince Charles went windsurfing. Stories that she lightheartedly tipped him off his surfboard do not ring true of Diana who was totally in awe of him. Indeed she felt "fairly intimidated" by the atmosphere on board the royal yacht. Not only were his friends so much older than herself, but they seemed aware of Prince Charles's strategy towards her. She found them too friendly and too knowing. "They were all over me like a bad rash," she told her friends. For a girl who likes to be in control it was profoundly disconcerting.

There was little time to reflect on the implications as Prince Charles had already asked her to Balmoral for the weekend of the Braemar Games early in September. The Queen's Highland castle retreat, set in 40,000 acres of heather and grouse moor, is effectively the Windsors' family seat. Ever since Queen Victoria bought the estate in 1848 it has had a special place in the affections of the royal family. However the very quirks and obscure family traditions which have accrued over the years can intimidate newcomers. "Don't sit there" they chorus at an unfortunate guest foolish enough to try and sit in a chair in the drawing-room which was last used by Queen Victoria. Those who successfully navigate this social minefield, popularly known as "the Balmoral test", are accepted by the royal family. The ones who fail vanish from royal favour as quickly as the Highland mists come and go.

So the prospect of her stay at Balmoral loomed large in Diana's mind. She was "terrified" and desperately wanted to behave in the appropriate manner. Fortunately rather than staying in the main house, she was able to stay with her sister Jane and husband Robert who, as he was a member of the royal Household, enjoyed a grace and favour cottage on the estate. Prince Charles rang her every day, suggesting she join him for a walk or a barbecue.

It was a "wonderful" few days until the glint of a pair of binoculars across the river Dee spoilt their idyll. They were carried by royal journalist James Whitaker who had spotted Prince Charles fishing by the banks of the river Dee. The hunters had become the hunted. Diana immediately told Charles that she would make herself scarce so while he continued fishing she hid behind a tree for half an hour hoping vainly that the journalists would go away. Cleverly she used the mirror from her powder compact to watch the unholy trinity of James Whitaker and rival photographers Ken Lennox and Arthur Edwards as they tried to capture her on film. She foiled their efforts by calmly walking straight up through the pine trees, her head muffled with a headscarf and flat cap, leaving Fleet Street's finest clueless as to her identity.

They soon picked up her trail and from then on her private life was effectively over. Reporters waited outside her apartment day and night, while photographers badgered her at the Young England kindergarten where she worked. On one occasion she agreed to pose for photographs on the condition that she would then be left alone. Unfortunately during the photo session the light was behind her and made her cotton skirt seem see-through, revealing her legs to the world. "I knew your legs were good but I didn't realize they were that spectacular," Prince Charles is reported to have commented. "And did you really have to show them to everybody?"

While Prince Charles could afford to be amused, Diana was quickly discovering the exacting price of royal romance. She was telephoned in the early hours of the morning about stories in newspapers and yet dare not take the communal telephone off the hook in case any of their families became ill during the night. Each time she went out in her distinctive red Metro she was followed by a press posse. However she never lost control, giving polite but non-committal answers to endless questions about her feelings for the Prince. Her engaging smile, her winsome manner and her impeccable behaviour soon endeared her to the public. Her flatmate Carolyn Bartholomew says: "She played it just right. She didn't in any way splash it across the newspapers because that ruined her sister's chances. Diana was very aware that if anything special had to be cultivated it should take place without any pressure from the press."

Nonetheless, there was constant stress which tested her reserves to the limit. In the privacy of her apartment she could afford to show her feelings. "I cried like a baby to the four walls, I just couldn't cope with it," she recalls. Prince Charles never offered to help and when, in desperation, she contacted the press office at Buckingham Palace, they told her that she was on her own. While they washed their hands of any involvement, Diana dipped deep into her inner resources, drawing upon her instinctive determination to survive.

What made it worse was that Prince Charles seemed less concerned about her predicament than that of his friend Camilla Parker-Bowles. When he called Diana on the phone he often spoke in sympathetic tones about the rough time Camilla was getting because there were three or four journalists outside her home.

Diana bit her lip and said nothing, never mentioning the virtual siege she was living under. She didn't think that it was her place to do so nor did she want to appear to be a burden to the man she loved.

As the romance gathered momentum, Diana began to harbour doubts about her new friend Camilla Parker-Bowles. She seemed to know everything that Diana and Charles had discussed in their rare moments of privacy and was full of advice on how best to handle Prince Charles. It was all very strange. Even Diana, an absolute beginner in the rules of love, was starting to suspect that this was not the way most men conducted their romances. For a start she and Charles were never on their own. At her first Balmoral when she stayed with her sister Jane, the Parker-Bowleses were prominent among the house guests. When Charles invited her to dine at Buckingham Palace the Parker-Bowleses or his skiing companions Charles and Patti Palmer-Tomkinson were always present.

On October 24, 1980 when Diana drove from London to Ludlow to watch Prince Charles race his horse Allibar in the Clun Handicap for amateur riders they spent the weekend with the Parker-Bowleses at Bolehyde Manor in Wiltshire. The following day Charles and Andrew Parker-Bowles went out with the Beaufort Hunt while Camilla and Diana spent the morning together. They made a return visit to Bolehyde Manor the following weekend.

During that first weekend Prince Charles showed Diana around Highgrove, the 353-acre Gloucestershire home he had bought in July — the same month he had started to woo her. As he took her on a guided tour of the eight-bedroomed mansion, the Prince asked her to organize the interior decoration. He liked her taste while she felt that it was a "most improper" suggestion as they were not even engaged.

So Diana was deeply distressed when the *Sunday Mirror* newspaper ran a front page story claiming that, on November 5, Diana drove from London for a secret meeting with Prince Charles aboard the royal train in a siding at Holt in Wiltshire. For once Buckingham Palace came to her assistance. The Queen authorized her press secretary to demand a retraction. There was an exchange of letters which the editor, Bob Edwards, published coincidentally on the same day that Prince Charles flew to India and Nepal for an official tour. Diana insisted that she had been in her apartment, exhausted after a late night at the Ritz hotel where she and Prince Charles had attended Princess Margaret's 50th birthday party. "The whole thing has got out of control, I'm not so much bored as miserable," confided Diana to a sympathetic neighbour who just happened to be a journalist.

Her mother, Frances Shand Kydd also took the opportunity to enter the fray on behalf of her youngest daughter. In early December she wrote a letter to *The Times* complaining about the lies and harassment Diana had endured since the romance became public.

"May I ask the editors of Fleet Street, whether, in the execution of their jobs, they consider it necessary or fair to harass my daughter daily, from dawn until well after dusk? Is it fair to ask any human being, regardless of circumstances, to be treated in this way?" While her letter galvanized sixty Members of Parliament to draft a motion "deploring the manner in which Lady Diana Spencer is being treated by the media" and led to a meeting between editors and the Press Council, the seige of Coleherne Court continued.

Sandringham, the royal family's winter fortress, was also surrounded by the media. The House of Windsor, protected by police, press secretaries, and endless private acres, showed less composure than the House of Spencer. The Queen shouted: "Why don't you go away?" at the crowd of hacks while Prince Charles heckled: "A very happy New Year, and to your editors a particularly nasty one!" Prince Edward is even said to have fired a shotgun over the head of a *Daily Mirror* photographer.

Back at Coleherne Court, the beleaguered garrison managed to outwit the enemy when it mattered. On one occasion, when Diana was due to stay with Prince Charles at Broadlands, she stripped the sheets from her bed and used them to lower her suitcase from the kitchen window to the street below, out of sight of the waiting newshounds. On another occasion she climbed over dustbins and went through the fire exit of a Knightsbridge store, while once she and Carolyn abandoned her car and jumped on a red double decker bus to evade photographers. When the bus got caught in traffic they dashed off it and ran through a nearby Russell and Bromley shoe store. "That was brilliant fun," says Carolyn, "like being on a drag hunt in the middle of London."

They had organized a decoy system whereby Carolyn drove Diana's car to entice her press pursuers away and then Diana would emerge from Coleherne Court and walk off in the other direction. Even her grandmother, Lady Fermoy, joined in the subterfuge. Diana, having spent Christmas 1980 at Althorp, returned to London to spend New Year's Eve with her flatmates. The next day she drove to Sandringham but first left her distinctive Metro at Kensington Palace where her grandmother's silver VW Golf was waiting. Away she went in the VW, leaving the gentlemen of the press behind.

As the hysterical media juggernaut pushed Charles and Diana along to the altar, she had to try and come to terms with her own feelings and thoughts about the Prince of Wales. It was not easy. She had never had a real boyfriend before and so had no yardstick by which to compare Charles's behaviour. During their bizarre courtship she was his willing puppy who came to heel when he whistled. It was no more than he expected. As the Prince of Wales, he was used to being the centre of attention and the focus of flattery and praise. He called her Diana, she addressed him as "Sir".

He aroused her mothering instincts. When she came back from a date with the Prince she would be full of sympathy for him uttering phrases like "they work him too hard" or "it's appalling the way they push him around". In her eyes he was a sad, lonely man who needed looking after. And she was hopelessly, utterly besotted with him. He was the man she wanted to be with for the rest of her life and she was willing to jump through any hoop and over any hurdle to win him. Diana regularly asked

110

her flatmates for advice on how she should conduct her romance. As Carolyn recalls: "It was pretty normal procedure that goes on between girls. Some of it I can't disclose, some of it would have been on the lines of: 'Make sure you do this or that.' It was a bit of a game."

As she bathed in the warm glow of first love, she was occasionally unsettled by shards of doubt. Surprisingly, it was her grandmother, Ruth, Lady Fermoy, a lady-in-waiting to the Queen Mother, who sounded one of the first notes of caution. Far from engineering the union, as has been widely suspected, her grandmother advised her about the difficulties of marrying into the royal family. "You must understand that their sense of humour and lifestyle are very different," she warned her. "I don't think it will suit you."

Diana was also troubled by other worries. There was his clique of sycophantic friends, many of them middle-aged, who were too fawning and deferential. She instinctively felt that that kind of attention wasn't good for him. Then there was the ever-present Mrs Parker-Bowles who seemed to know everything they were doing almost before they had done it. During their courtship Diana had asked him about his previous girlfriends. He had told her candidly that they were married women because, in his words, "they were safe". They had their husbands to think about and so would never dare talk. Yet Diana truly believed he was in love with her because of the devoted way he behaved in her presence. At the same time she couldn't help but wonder about the fact that in the space of twelve months he had been involved in three relationships, Anna Wallace, Amanda Knatchbull and herself, any one of which could have ended in marriage.

Those doubts disappeared following a telephone call she received while Prince Charles was on a skiing holiday in Klosters, Switzerland. During his call, made from the chalet of his friends Charles and Patti Palmer-Tomkinson, he said that he had something important to ask her when he returned. Instinct told her what that "something" was and that night she talked until the small hours with her flatmates discussing what she should do. She was in love, she thought he was in love with her and yet she was aware that there was another woman, Camilla Parker-Bowles, hovering in the background.

He returned to England on February 3, 1981, looking fit and tanned. That Thursday he joined HMS *Invincible*, the Royal Navy's latest aircraft carrier, for manoeuvres, and returned to London where he spent the night at Buckingham Palace. He had arranged to see Diana the following day, Friday February 6, at Windsor Castle. It was here that the Prince of Wales formally asked Lady Diana Spencer to be his bride.

The actual proposal took place late that evening in the Windsor nursery. He told her how much he had missed her while he was away skiing and then asked her simply to marry him. At first she treated his request in a light-hearted way and broke into a fit of giggles. The Prince was deadly serious, emphasizing the earnestness of his proposal by reminding her that one day she would be queen. While a small voice inside her head told her that she would never become queen but would have a tough life she found herself accepting his offer and telling him repeatedly how much she loved him. "Whatever love means", he replied, a phrase he was to use again during their formal engagement interviews with the media.

He left her and went upstairs to telephone the Queen, who was at Sandringham, and inform her of the happy outcome of his proposal. In the meantime Diana pondered her fate. Despite her nervous laughter, Diana had given the prospect much thought. Besides her undoubted love for Prince Charles, her sense of duty and her deep desire to carry out a useful role in life were factors in her fateful decision.

When she returned to her apartment later that night her friends were eager for news. She flopped down on her bed and announced: "Guess what?" They cried out in unison: "He asked you." Diana replied: "He did and I said: 'Yes please.' " After the congratulatory hugs and tears and kisses, they opened a bottle of champagne before they went for a drive round London nursing their secret.

She told her parents the next day. They were naturally thrilled but when she told her brother Charles of her marriage plans at their mother's London apartment he wisecracked: "Who to?" He recalls: "When I got there she looked absolutely blissful and was beaming away. I just remember her as really ecstatic." Did he feel then that she was in love with the role or the person? "From the baptism of fire she had got from the press she knew that she could handle the role too. She looked as happy as I have ever seen her look. It was genuine because nobody with insincere motives could look that happy. It wasn't the look of somebody who had won the jackpot but somebody who looked spiritually fulfilled as well."

Her sister Sarah, for so long the Spencer girl in the spotlight, now had to make way for Diana. While she was happy for her younger sister, she admitted to being rather envious of Diana's new found fame. It took her some time to adjust to her new billing as sister to the future Princess of Wales. Jane took a more practical approach. While she shared in the bride-to-be's euphoria, as the wife of the Queen's assistant private secretary, she couldn't help but be concerned about how Diana would cope with royal life.

This was for the future. Two days later Diana took a well-earned break, her last as a private citizen. She joined her mother and stepfather on a flight for Australia where they travelled to his sheep station at Yass in New South Wales. They stayed at a friend's beach house and enjoyed ten days of peace and seclusion.

While Diana and her mother started planning guest lists, wardrobe requirements and the other details for the wedding of the year, the media vainly attempted to discover her hiding-place. The one man who did know was the Prince of Wales. As the days passed, Diana pined for her Prince and yet he never telephoned. She excused his silence as due to the pressure of his royal duties. Finally she called him only to find that he was not in his apartment at Buckingham Palace. It was only after she called him that he telephoned her. Soothed by that solitary telephone call, Diana's ruffled pride was momentarily mollified when she returned to Coleherne Court. There was a knock on the door and a member of the Prince's staff appeared with a large bouquet of flowers. However there was no note from her future husband and she concluded sadly that it was simply a tactful gesture by his office.

These concerns were forgotten a few days later when Diana rose at dawn and travelled to the Lambourn home of Nick Gaselee, Charles's trainer, to watch him ride his horse, Allibar. As she and his detective observed the Prince put the horse through its paces on the gallops Diana was seized by another premonition of disaster. She said that Allibar was going to have a heart attack and die. Within seconds of her uttering those words, 11-year-old Allibar reared its head back and collapsed to the ground with a massive coronary. Diana leapt out of the Land Rover and raced to Charles's side. There was nothing anyone could do. The couple stayed with the horse until a vet officially certified its death and then, to avoid waiting photographers, Diana left the Gaselees in the back of the Land Rover with a coat over her head.

It was a miserable moment but there was little time to reflect on the tragedy. The inexorable demands of royal duty took Prince Charles on to Wales, leaving Diana to sympathize with his loss by telephone. Soon they would be together forever, the subterfuge and deceit ended. It was nearly time to let the world into their secret.

The night before the engagement announcement, which took place on February 24, 1981, she packed a bag, hugged her loyal friends and left Coleherne Court forever. She had an armed Scotland Yard bodyguard for company, Chief Inspector Paul Officer, a philosophical policeman who is fascinated by runes, mysticism and the after-world. As she prepared to say goodbye to her private life, he told her: "I just want you to know that this is the last night of freedom in your life so make the most of it."

Those words stopped her in her tracks. "They felt like a sword through my heart."

4

"Such Hope in My Heart"

The quest of the handsome prince was complete. He had found his fair maiden and the world had its fairytale. In her ivory tower, Cinderella was unhappy, locked away from her friends, her family and the outside world. As the public celebrated the Prince's fortune, the shades of the prison-house closed inexorably around Diana.

For all her aristocratic breeding, this innocent young kindergarten teacher felt totally at sea in the deferential hierarchy of Buckingham Palace. There were many tears in those three months and many more to come after that. Weight simply dropped off, her waist shrinking from 29 inches when the engagement was announced down to 23 inches on her wedding day. It was during this turbulent time that her bulimia nervosa, which would take nearly a decade to overcome, began. The note Diana left her friends at Coleherne Court said: "For God's sake ring me up — I'm going to need you." It proved painfully accurate.

As Carolyn Bartholomew, who watched her waste away during her engagement, recalls: "She went to live at Buckingham Palace and then the tears started. This little thing got so thin. I was so worried about her. She wasn't happy, she was suddenly plunged into all this pressure and it was a nightmare for her. She was dizzy with it, bombarded from all sides. It was a whirlwind and she was ashen, she was grey."

Her first night at Clarence House, the Queen Mother's London residence, was the calm before the coming storm. She was left to her own devices when she arrived, no-one from the royal family, least of all her future husband, thinking it necessary to welcome her to her new world. The popular myth paints a homely picture of the Queen Mother clucking around Diana as she schooled her in the subtle arts of royal protocol while the Queen's senior lady-in-waiting, Lady Susan Hussey, took the young woman aside for tuition in regal history. In reality, Diana was given less training in her new job than the average supermarket checkout operator.

Diana was shown to her first-floor bedroom by a servant. There was a letter lying on her bed. It was from Camilla Parker-Bowles and had been written several days before the engagement was officially announced. The friendly note invited her to lunch. It was during that meeting, arranged to coincide with Prince Charles's trip to Australia and New Zealand, that Diana began to see the way Camilla's mind was working. She kept asking if Diana was going to hunt when she moved to Highgrove. Nonplussed by such an odd question, Diana replied in the negative. The relief on Camilla's face was clear. Diana later realized that her rival saw Charles's love of hunting as a conduit to maintaining her own relationship.

It wasn't clear at the time. Then again nothing was. Diana soon moved into rooms at Buckingham Palace where she, her mother and a small team had to organize her wedding and her wardrobe. Diana quickly appreciated that the only thing the royal family like to change is their clothes. With the year divided into three official seasons and often involving four formal changes of clothes a day, her wardrobe of one long dress, one silk shirt and a smart pair of shoes was wholly inadequate. During her romance she had regularly raided her friends' wardrobes so that she would have a presentable outfit to go out in. While her mother helped her choose the famous blue engagement suit which she bought from Harrods, she asked her sisters' friend Anna Harvey, the fashion editor of *Vogue* magazine, for advice on building up her formal wardrobe.

She began to understand that her working clothes had not just to be fashionable but also to cope with the vagaries of walkabouts, the intrusion of photographers and her ever-present enemy, the wind. Slowly she discovered tricks of the trade such as weighting her hems so that they didn't blow up in a breeze and she gradually acquired a coterie of designers, including Catherine Walker, David Sassoon and Victor Edelstein, whom she now relies upon.

At first there was no grand plan, it was simply a case of choosing who was around or who had been recommended by her new friends from *Vogue*. She picked two young designers, David and Elizabeth Emanuel, to make the wedding-dress because she was impressed by their work when she attended a photographic shoot at Lord Snowdon's Kensington studio. They also made the evening gown for her first official engagement, a charity gala in the City of London, which created almost as big a sensation as the dress which graced St Paul's Cathedral a few months later.

The black taffeta silk ballgown was strapless and backless with a plunging, gravity-defying decolletage. Prince Charles was not impressed with the outfit. While she thought black was the smartest colour a girl her age could wear, he had different ideas. When she appeared in her finery at the door of his study he commented unfavorably saying that only people in mourning wore black. Diana replied that she was not yet a member of his family and, what's more, she had no other dress suitable for the occasion.

That spat did little for her confidence as she faced a battery of cameras waiting outside Goldsmiths Hall. She was unschooled in the niceties of royal behaviour and felt absolutely terrified that she would embarrass her fiancé in some way. "It was an horrendous occasion," she told her friends. During the course of the evening she met Princess Grace of Monaco, a woman she had always admired from afar.

She noticed Diana's uncertainty and, ignoring the other guests who were still buzzing over Diana's choice of dress, whisked her off to the powder room. Diana poured her heart out about the publicity, her sense of isolation and fears about what the future held in store. "Don't worry," Princess Grace joked. "It will get a lot worse."

At the end of that momentous month of March, Prince Charles flew to Australia for a five-week visit. Before he climbed the gangway of the RAF VC10 he grasped her arm and kissed her on each cheek. As she watched his plane taxi away, she broke down and wept. This vulnerability further endeared her to the public. However, her tears were not what they seemed. Before he had left for the airport, he had attended to a few last minute details in his study at Buckingham Palace. Diana was chatting to him when the telephone rang. It was Camilla. Diana wondered whether to sit there or leave and let them make their farewells in private. She left her fiancé alone but told friends afterwards that the episode broke her heart.

She was now alone in the ivory tower. For a girl used to the noise and chaos of an all girls' apartment, Buckingham Palace felt like anywhere but home. Diana found it a place of "dead energy" and grew to despise the smooth evasions and subtle equivocations employed by courtiers, particularly when she asked them directly about her fiancé's relationship with Camilla Parker-Bowles. Lonely and feeling sorry for herself, she regularly wandered from her second floor apartment to the kitchens to chat to the staff. On one famous occasion Diana, barefoot and casually dressed in jeans, buttered toast for an astonished footman.

She found some solace in her love of dancing, inviting the West Heath school pianist, the late Lily Snipp and Wendy Mitchell, her dance teacher, to Buckingham Palace to give her private lessons. For forty minutes Diana, dressed in a black leotard, went through a routine that combined ballet with tap dancing.

During those momentous days Miss Snipp kept a diary which gives a first-hand feeling of the misgivings felt by Lady Diana Spencer as the wedding-day approached. The first entry in Miss Snipp's diary, on Friday June 5, 1981, recorded details of Diana's first lesson. She wrote: "To Buckingham Palace to play for Lady Diana. We all worked hard at the lesson, no time wasted. When the lesson was over Lady Diana, with her tongue in her cheek, said: 'I suppose Miss Snipp will now go direct to Fleet Street.' She has a good sense of humour — she will need it in the years to come."

The most poignant lesson, which proved to be the last, was held a few days before the wedding. Diana's thoughts were on the profound changes ahead. Miss Snipp noted: "Lady Diana rather tired — too many late nights. I delivered silver salt-cellars — present from West Heath school — very beautiful and much admired. Lady Diana counting how many days of freedom are left to her. Rather sad. Masses of people outside of Palace. We hope to resume lessons in October. Lady Diana said: 'In 12 days time I shall no longer be me.'"

Even as she spoke those words Diana must have known that she had left behind her bachelor *persona* as soon as she had entered the Palace portals. In the weeks following the engagement she had grown in confidence and self-assurance, her sense of humour frequently bubbling to the surface. Lucinda Craig Harvey saw her former cleaning lady on several occasions during her engagement, once at the 30th birthday party of her brother-in-law, Neil McCorquodale. "She had a distance to her and everyone was in awe of her," she recalls. It was a quality also noticed by James Gilbey. "She has always been seen as a typical Sloane Ranger. That's not true. She was always removed, always had a determination about her and was very matter-of-fact, almost dogmatic. That quality has now developed into a tremendous presence."

While she was in awe of Prince Charles, deferring to his every decision, she didn't appear to be overcome by her surroundings. Inwardly she may have been nervous, outwardly she appeared calm, relaxed and ready to have fun. At Prince Andrew's 21st birthday party which was held at Windsor Castle she was at her ease among friends. When her future brother-in-law asked where he could find the Duchess of Westminster, the wife of Britain's richest aristocrat, she joked: "Oh Andrew, do stop name dropping." Her ready repartee, cutting but not vicious, was reminiscent of her eldest sister Sarah when she was the queen bee of the Society circuit.

"Don't look so serious, it's not working," joked Diana as she introduced Adam Russell to the Queen, Prince Charles and other members of the royal family in the receiving line at the ball held at Buckingham Palace two days before her wedding. Once again she seemed good humoured and relaxed in her grand surroundings. There wasn't the slightest sign that a few hours earlier she had collapsed in paroxysms of tears and seriously considered calling the whole thing off.

The cause of the tears was the arrival, a few days earlier, of a parcel at the busy Buckingham Palace office which she shared with Michael Colbourne, who was then in charge of the Prince's finances, and several others. Diana insisted on opening it, despite firm remonstratations from the Prince's right hand man. Inside was a gold chain bracelet with a blue enamel disc and the initials "F" and "G" entwined. The initials stand for "Fred" and "Gladys", the nicknames used by Camilla and Charles which Diana had been made aware of by friends. It had come home to her earlier when she discovered that the Prince had sent a bouquet of flowers to Camilla when she had been ill. Once again he used that affectionate nickname.

Work in the Prince's office at Buckingham Palace came to a halt when Diana confronted her husband-to-be about his proposed gift. In spite of her angry and tearful protests Charles insisted on giving the token to the woman who had haunted their courtship and has since cast a long shadow across their married life. The full enormity of the charade hit her a week before the wedding when she attended a rehearsal at St Paul's Cathedral. As soon as the camera lights were switched on, it triggered the churning emotions in her heart and she broke down and wept inconsolably.

The public glimpsed her frustration and desperation the weekend before the wedding when she left a polo field at Tidworth in floods of tears. By then, though, the television cameras were in place for the wedding, the cake had been baked, the crowds were already gathering on the pavement and the sense of happy anticipation was almost palpable. On the Monday before her wedding-day, Diana gave serious consideration to calling a halt to the whole affair. At lunchtime she knew that Prince Charles had gone to present Camilla with her gift, even leaving behind his senior bodyguard, Chief Inspector John McLean.

At the time he was seeing Camilla, Diana

127

had lunch with her sisters at Buckingham Palace and discussed her predicament with them. She was confused, upset and bewildered by the train of events. At that moment, as she seriously considered calling-off the wedding, they made light of her fears and premonitions of the disaster which lay ahead. "Bad luck, Duch," they said, using the family nickname for their younger sister, "your face is on the tea-towels so you're too late to chicken out now."

Her head and heart were in turmoil but no-one would have guessed it when later that evening she and Charles entertained 800 of their friends and family at a ball inside Buckingham Palace. It was a memorable night of riotous jollity. Princess Margaret attached a balloon to her tiara, Prince Andrew tied another to the tails of his dinner jacket while royal bar staff dispensed a cocktail called "A Long Slow Comfortable Screw up against the Throne". Rory Scott recalls dancing with Diana in front of the then Prime Minister, Margaret Thatcher, and embarrassing himself by continually standing on Diana's toes.

The comedian Spike Milligan held forth about God, Diana gave a priceless diamond and pearl necklace to a friend to look after while she danced; while the Queen was observed looking through the programme and saying in bemused tones: "It says here they have live music", as though it had just been invented. Diana's brother, Charles, just down from Eton, vividly remembers bowing to one of the waiters. "He was absolutely weighed down with medals," he recalls, "and by that stage, with so many royal people there, I was in automatic bowing mode. I bowed and he looked surprised. Then he asked me if I wanted a drink."

For most of the guests the evening passed in a haze of euphoria. "It was an intoxicatingly happy atmosphere," recalls Adam Russell. "Everyone horribly drunk and then catching taxis in the early hours, it was a blur, a glorious, happy blur."

On the eve of the wedding, which Diana spent at Clarence House, her mood was much improved when Charles sent her a signet ring engraved with the Prince of Wales feathers and an affectionate card which said: "I'm so proud of you and when you come up I'll be there at the altar for you tomorrow. Just look 'em in the eye and knock 'em dead."

While his loving note helped to sooth her misgivings, it was difficult to control the inner turmoil which had been building up over the months. During dinner that evening with her sister Jane, she ate everything she could and then was promptly sick. The stress and tension of the occasion were partly to blame but the incident was also an early symptom of bulimia nervosa, the illness which took pernicious hold later that year. She has since told a close friend: "The night before the wedding I was very calm, deathly calm. I felt I was the lamb to the slaughter. I knew it and I couldn't do anything about it."

She woke early on the morning of July 29, 1981 which is not surprising as her room overlooked the Mall where the singing, chattering crowds had been gathering for days. It was the start of what she later described as "the most emotionally confusing day of my life." Listening to the crowds outside, she felt a deathly composure combined with great anticipation at the event which lay ahead.

Her hairdresser Kevin Shanley, make-up artist Barbara Daly and David and Elizabeth Emanuel were on hand to ensure that the bride looked her best. They succeeded. Her brother Charles remembers his sister's transformation. "She was never one for make-up but she did look fantastic. It was the first time in my life I ever thought of Diana as beautiful. She really did look stunning that day and very composed, not showing any nerves although she was slightly pale. She was happy and calm."

Her father, who gave her away, was thrilled. "Darling, I'm so proud of you," he said as she walked down the staircase at Clarence House. As she climbed in to the Glass Coach with her father, Diana had several practical considerations to overcome. Her dressmakers realized too late that they had not taken the size of the coach into consideration when they had designed the ivory silk wedding gown with its 25-foot-long train. In spite of all Diana's effort it was badly crushed in the short journey to St Paul's.

She also knew that it was her priority to get her father, physically impaired since his stroke, down the aisle. "It was a deeply moving moment for us when he made it," observes Charles Spencer. Earl Spencer loved the carriage ride, waving enthusiastically to the crowds. As they reached St Martin-in-the-Fields church the cheering was so loud he thought that they had arrived at St Paul's and prepared to get out of the carriage.

When they finally arrived at the cathedral, the world held its collective breath and Diana, with her father leaning heavily on her arm, walked with painful slowness down the aisle. Diana had plenty of time to spot the guests, who included Camilla Parker-Bowles. As she walked down the aisle her heart brimmed over with love and adoration for Charles. When she looked at him through her veil her fears vanished and she thought that she was the luckiest girl in the world. She had such hope for the future, such belief that he would love, nurture and protect her from the difficulties that lay ahead. That moment was watched by 750 million people gathered around television sets in more than seventy countries. It was, in the words of the Archbishop of Canterbury, "the stuff of which fairy-tales are made".

But for the moment she had to concentrate on dipping a formal curtsey to the Queen, a consideration which had greatly exercised her mind in the previous few days. When the newly created Princess of Wales emerged from St Paul's Cathedral to the cheers of the crowd, hope and happiness brimmed in her heart. She convinced herself that the bulimia, which had scarred her engagement, was simply an attack of pre-wedding nerves and that Mrs Parker-Bowles was consigned to history. She now speaks of those hours of heady emotion in a voice of wry amusement: "I had tremendous hopes in my heart."

She was proved bitterly wrong. The relationship between Prince Charles and Camilla continues to this day and could still be the catalyst which changes the course of British royal history. In Diana's mind this unworkable emotional triangle has engendered a decade of angst, anguish and anger. There are no winners. A friend of both of them, who has watched this unhappy saga unfold over the last decade, now concedes: "I am sorry for the tragedy of it all. My heart bleeds for the whole misunderstanding but it bleeds most for Diana."

But on that July day, Diana basked in the warm affection of the crowds who lined the route back to Buckingham Palace where the royal family and their guests enjoyed the traditional royal wedding-breakfast. By then she was simply too weary to think clearly, feeling totally overwhelmed by the spontaneous display of affection from the patriotic crowd.

She was longing for some peace and privacy, believing that now the wedding was over she would slip back into relative obscurity. The royal couple found that seclusion at Broadlands, Earl Mountbatten's home in Hampshire, where they spent the first three days of their honeymoon, followed by a leisurely Mediterranean cruise on board the royal yacht *Britannia* which they joined at Gibraltar. Prince Charles had his own ideas about married life. He brought along his fishing tackle which he used at their Hampshire retreat, together with half a dozen books by his friend and mentor, the South African philosopher and adventurer, Sir Laurens van der Post. It was his idea that they should read his books together and then discuss van der Post's mystical ideas at mealtimes.

Diana, on the other hand, wanted to spend time really getting to know her husband. For much of their engagement his royal duties had taken him away from her side. On board the royal yacht, with its 21 officers and 256 men, they were never left alone. Evening meals were black-tie affairs attended by selected officers. While they discussed the day's events, a Royal Marine band played in an adjoining room. The nervous tension of the build-up to the wedding had left the royal couple absolutely drained. For much of the time they slept and when she wasn't sleeping Diana frequently visited the kitchens, the domain of "Swampie" Marsh and fellow chefs. They were amused by the way she consumed endless bowls of ice-cream or asked them to make her special snacks in between the normal meals.

Over the years royal staff and her friends have been puzzled by Diana's appetite, particularly as she always appeared to be so slim. She was frequently found raiding the refrigerator at Highgrove late in the evening, and once startled a footman by eating an entire steak and kidney pie when she was staying at Windsor Castle. Her friend Rory Scott remembers her eating a 1lb bag of sweets in short order during a bridge evening while her admission that she ate a bowl of custard before she went to bed added to the perplexity concerning her diet.

In fact, virtually from the moment she became the Princess of Wales, Diana has suffered from bulimia nervosa which helps to explain her erratic dietary behaviour. As Carolyn Bartholomew, who has been instrumental in convincing Diana to seek medical help, observes: "It's been there through her royal career, without a doubt. I hate to say it but I feel that it may erupt when she feels under pressure." Bulimia, according to a recent Drug and Therapeutics bulletin from the Consumers' Association, is suffered by around two percent of young women in Britain. These women indulge in episodes of massive overeating associated with a sense of loss of control. Between episodes of eating most sufferers fast or induce vomiting. Binges tend to be secret, sometimes pre-planned and are often followed by strong mood swings expressed as guilt, depression, self-hate and even suicidal behaviour. Sufferers usually have a normal body weight but see themselves as being fat, bloated and ugly. This dislike of their bodies leads to fasting between the episodes of overeating and sufferers commonly have a sense of failure, low self-esteem and loss of control. Muscle cramps, kidney and even heart failure are the physical results of prolonged bulimia.

Unlike anorexia nervosa, bulimia survives by disguise. It is a sophisticated illness in as much as sufferers do not admit that they have a problem. They always appear to be happy and spend their lives trying to help others. Yet there is rage beneath the sunny smile, anger which sufferers are afraid to express. Women in the caring professions such as nursing and nannying are particularly prone to the illness. They see their own needs as greed and subsequently feel guilty about caring for themselves. That disgust is translated into violent purging by vomiting or laxatives. As the medical bulletin concludes: "Bulimia nervosa is a serious, under-recognized, potentially chronic and occasionally fatal disorder affecting many young women but rarely men."

While the roots of both bulimia and anorexia lie in childhood and a disordered family background, uncertainty and anxiety in adult life provide the trigger for the illness. For Diana, the last few months had been an emotional rollercoaster as she had tried to come to terms with her new life as a public figure and the suffocating publicity as well as her husband's friends and his ambiguous behaviour towards her. It was an explosive cocktail and it took just one spark to bring on her illness. On one occasion, as the wedding day drew near,

Charles put his arm around her waist and commented on what he considered to be her chubby figure. It was an innocent enough remark but it triggered something inside her. Shortly afterwards she made herself sick. It was a profound release of tension and in some hazy way gave her a sense of control over herself and a means of releasing the anger she felt.

Their honeymoon gave no respite. In fact it became much worse as Diana would make herself sick four, sometimes five times a day. The ever-present shadow cast by Camilla merely served to throw fuel on the flames. Reminders were everywhere. On one occasion they were comparing engagements in their respective diaries when two photographs of Camilla fell out from the pages of Charles's diary. Amid the tears and the angry words, she pleaded with him to be honest about how he felt about her and Camilla. Those words fell on deaf ears. Several days later they entertained the Egyptian President, Anwar Sadat, and his wife Jihan on board the royal yacht. When Charles appeared for dinner, Diana noticed that he was sporting a new pair of cufflinks in the shape of two "C"s intertwined. He admitted that they were from Camilla but passed them off as a simple gesture of friendship. Diana didn't see it that way. As she commented angrily to friends later, she could not see why Charles needed these constant reminders of Camilla.

In public however Diana appeared buoyant and happy. She joined in a singsong in the sailors' mess, playing "What shall we do with a drunken sailor?" after drinking from a can of beer. "We were all tickled pink," recalls one sailor. One moonlit night they enjoyed a barbecue in a bay on the coast of Ithaca. It was organized by the yacht's officers, who did all the cooking. After they had eaten, a Royal Marine accordionist came ashore, song sheets were handed out, and the night air rang to the sound of Boy Scout songs and sea chanties.

In its own way, the honeymoon finale was the highpoint of the trip. For days the officers and men had rehearsed a farewell concert. There were more than fourteen acts, from stand-up comics to bawdy singalongs. The royal couple returned to Britain looking fit, tanned and very much in love and flew to join the Queen and the rest of the royal family on the Balmoral estate.

But the Highland mists did little to soothe Diana's troubled spirit. Indeed when they arrived at Balmoral, where they stayed from August to late October, the full impact of life as Princess of Wales began to hit home. She had believed, like many others in the royal family, that her fame would be transitory, her star soon fading following the wedding. Everyone, even newspaper editors, were caught unawares by the Princess Diana phenomenon. Their readers could not get enough of Diana; her face was on every magazine cover, every aspect of her life attracted comment and anyone who had ever known her was tracked down by the voracious media to be interviewed.

In a little under a year this insecure High School drop-out had undergone a process of deification by press and public. Her very ordinariness was celebrated; everyday gestures such as opening a car door herself or buying a bag of sweets were acclaimed as evidence of a very human princess. Everyone was infected, even the royal family's guests at Balmoral that autumn. Diana was profoundly confused. She had not altered overmuch in the twelve months since she was covering cars with eggs and flour and ringing doorbells with her giggling friends.

As she mingled with the guests at the Queen's Scottish home she realised that she was no longer treated as a person but as a position, no longer a flesh and blood human being with thoughts and feelings but a symbol where the very title "Her Royal Highness, the

Princess of Wales" distanced her not only from the wider public but from those within the intimate royal circle. Protocol decreed that she should be addressed as "Your Royal Highness" on first reference and "Ma'am" thereafter. Of course everyone curtsied too. Diana was disconcerted. "Don't call me ma'am, call me Duch," she told a friend shortly after her marriage. But no matter how much she tried she could not prevent the shift in perceptions towards her.

She realized that everyone looked at her with new eyes, handling her like a precious piece of porcelain to be admired but not touched. Diana was treated with kid gloves when all she needed was some sensible advice, a cuddle and a consoling word. Yet the confused young woman that was the real Diana was in grave danger of drowning in the tidal wave of change which had turned her world upside-down. For the watching world, she smiled and laughed, seeming perfectly delighted with her husband and newfound status. At a famous photocall by the Bridge of Dee on the Balmoral estate, Diana told the assembled media that she could "highly recommend" married life. However, away from the cameras and microphones, the couple argued continually. Diana was always on edge, suspecting Camilla's presence in Charles's every action. At times she believed that he was seeking Camilla's advice about his marriage or making arrangements to see her. As a close friend commented: "They had shocking rows about her, real stinkers and I don't blame Diana one bit."

She lived on an emotional see-saw, her jealousy matched by a sublime devotion to Charles. Diana was still totally besotted with him and Charles, in his own way, in love with her. They went for long rambles around the hills which overlook Balmoral and as they lay in the heather he read out passages from books by the Swiss psychiatrist, Carl Jung, or Laurens van der Post. Charles was happy and if he was content, so was Diana. The touching love letters they exchanged are testimony to that growing bond of affection.

But these romantic interludes were mere pauses in Diana's worries about public life, anxieties which did little to subdue her bulimic condition. She was continually sick, her weight falling drastically until she had literally gone to "skin and bone". At this critical juncture in her life she felt that there was no-one in whom she could confide. She assumed, correctly, that the Queen and other members of the royal family would take her husband's side. In any event the royal family, both by training and inclination, shy away from emotional breast beating. They live in a world of contained feelings and regimented activity. It was assumed by them that Diana would somehow be able to assume their rigid code of behaviour overnight.

Nor did she feel she could approach her own family for assistance. Her parents and sisters were sympathetic but expected her to conform to the existing *status quo*. Her girl-friends, particularly her former flatmates, would have rallied round but she did not feel that she could inflict them with such a burden of responsibility. She sensed that, like the rest of the world, they wanted the royal fairy-tale to work. They believed in the myth and Diana could not bring herself to tell them the awful truth. She was terribly alone and dreadfully exposed. Inexorably her thoughts turned to suicide, not because she wanted to die but because she desperately wanted help.

Her husband took matters into his own hands by asking Laurens van der Post to come to Scotland to see what he could do. His ministrations had little effect so in early October she flew to London for professional counselling. She saw several doctors and psychologists at Buckingham Palace. They diagnosed various tranquilizers to calm her down and recover her equilibrium. However Diana vigorously fought against their advice. She knew in her heart that she did not need drugs, she needed rest, patience and understanding from those around her. Just as she was bombarded by voices telling her to accept the doctors' recommendations she discovered that she was pregnant. "Thank Heavens for William," she has since said as it meant she could now quite properly forsake the pills she was proferred by arguing that she did not want to risk physical or mental deformity in the baby she was carrying.

Her pregnancy was a reprieve. It was reprieve that would not last long.

5

"My Cries for Help"

The sound of voices raised in anger and hysterical sobbing could be plainly heard coming from the suite of rooms occupied by the Prince and Princess of Wales at Sandringham House. It was shortly after Christmas but there was little festive feeling between the royal couple. Diana was then three months' pregnant with Prince William and felt absolutely wretched. Her relationship with Prince Charles was rapidly unravelling. The Prince seemed incapable of understanding or wishing to comprehend the turmoil in Diana's life. She was suffering dreadfully from morning sickness, she was haunted by Camilla Parker-Bowles and she was desperately trying to accommodate herself to her new position and new family.

As she later told friends: "One minute I was a nobody, the next minute I was Princess of Wales, mother, media toy, member of this family and it was just too much for one person to handle." She had pleaded, cajoled and quarrelled violently as she tried to win the Prince's assistance. In vain. On that fateful January day

144

Above : Diana in a low-cut ballgown before a dance at Althorp in 1980.

Below : A weekend shooting party at Althorp where the Duke of Kent, pictured on Diana's right, was the guest of honour. Other members of the party included Mr and Mrs Robin Leigh Pemberton, Jane and Robert Fellowes, Harry Herbert, Humphrey Butler, Carolyn Bartholomew and Diana.

Left: Diana and her brother Charles, photographed by their father.

Below: Diana and Humphrey Butler, who later became an auctioneer at Christie's.

Left: Diana adopts an unusual pose on the bed-settee where she slept during her holiday in the chalet party organized by Simon Berry.

Below: Prince Charles enjoys a quiet moment with his friend Camilla Parker-Bowles after a polo match. *(Rex Features)*

in 1982, her first New Year within the royal family, she now threatened to take her own life. He accused her of crying wolf and prepared to go riding on the Sandringham estate. She was as good as her word. Standing on top of the wooden staircase she hurled herself to the ground, landing in a heap at the bottom.

The Queen Mother was one of the first to arrive on the scene. She was horrified, physically shaking with the shock of what she had witnessed. A local doctor was summoned while George Pinker, Diana's gynaecologist, travelled from London to visit his royal patient. Her husband simply dismissed her plight and carried on with his plan to go riding. Fortunately Diana was not seriously hurt by the fall although she did suffer severe bruising around her stomach. A full check up revealed that the foetus had not been injured.

The incident was one of many domestic crises which crowded in upon the royal couple in those tumultuous early days. At every turning point they put a greater distance between each other. As her friend James Gilbey observes of her suicide attempts: "They were messages of complete desperation. Please, please help." In the first years of their married life, Diana made several suicide bids and numerous threats. It should be emphasized that they were not serious attempts to take her life but cries for help.

On one occasion she threw herself against a glass display cabinet at Kensington Palace while on another she slashed at her wrists with a razor blade. Another time she cut herself with the serrated edge of a lemon slicer; on yet another occasion, during a heated argument with Prince Charles, she picked up a penknife lying on his dressing table and cut her chest and her thighs. Although she was bleeding her husband studiously scorned her. As ever he thought that she was faking her problems. Later on, her sister Jane, who saw her shortly afterwards, remarked on the score marks on her body. Jane was horrified when she learned the truth.

As Diana has since told friends: "They were desperate cries for help. I just needed time to adjust to my new position." One friend who watched their relationship deteriorate points to Prince Charles's disinterest and total lack of respect for her at a time when Diana badly needed help. "His indifference pushed her to the edge whereas he could have romanced her to the end of the world. They could have set the world alight. Through no fault of his own, because of his own ignorance, upbringing and lack of a whole relationship with anyone in his life, he instilled this hatred of herself."

This is a partisan appraisal. In the early days

of their marriage Prince Charles did, for a time, try to ease his wife into the royal routine. Her first big test was a three-day visit to Wales in October 1980. The crowds made it painfully obvious who was the new star of the show — the Princess of Wales. Charles was left apologizing for not having enough wives to go round. If he took one side of the street during a walkabout the crowd collectively groaned, it was his wife they had come to see. "I seem to do nothing but collect flowers these days," he said. "I know my role." Behind the smiles there were other muttered concerns. The first sight of the Princess on a rainswept quayside in Wales came as a shock to royal watchers. It was the first chance to see Diana close up since the long honeymoon and it was like looking at a different woman. She wasn't just slim, she was painfully thin.

She had lost weight before the wedding; that was only to be expected — but the girl moving through the crowds, shaking hands and accepting flowers, looked positively transparent. Diana was two months' pregnant — and feeling worse than she looked. She chose the wrong clothes for the torrential rain which followed their every move, she was wracked by severe morning sickness and absolutely overwhelmed by the crowds who turned out to see her.

Diana admits that she wasn't easy to handle during that baptism of fire. She was often in tears as they travelled to the various venues, telling her husband that she simply could not face the crowds. She didn't have the energy or the resources to cope with the prospect of meeting so many people. There were times, many times, when she longed to be back in her safe bachelor apartment with her jolly, uncomplicated friends.

While Prince Charles sympathized with his tearful wife he insisted that the royal roadshow had to go on. He was understandably apprehensive when Diana made her first speech partly in Welsh at Cardiff City Hall when she was presented with the Freedom of the City. While Diana passed that test with aplomb, she discovered another truism about royal life. However well she did, however hard she tried she never earned a word of praise from her husband, the royal family or their courtiers. In her vulnerable, lonely position a little applause would have worked wonders. "I remember her saying that she was trying so damn hard and all she needed was a pat on the back," recalls a friend. "But it wasn't forthcoming." Every day she fought back the waves of nausea in order to fulfill her public engagements. She had such a morbid fear of letting down her husband and the royal family "firm" that she performed her official duties when she was quite clearly unwell. On two occasions she had to cancel engagements, on others she looked pale and sickly, acutely aware that she was not helping her husband. At least after her pregnancy was officially announced on November 5, 1981 Diana could publicly discuss her condition. The weary Princess said: "Some days I feel terrible. No-one told me I would feel like I did." She confessed to a passion for bacon and tomato sandwiches and took to telephoning her friend, Sarah Ferguson, the daughter of Charles's polo manager Major Ronald Ferguson. The irrepressible redhead regularly left her job at a London art dealer and drove round to Buckingham Palace to cheer up the royal mother-to-be.

In private it was no better. She stalwartly refused to take any drugs, once again arguing that she could not hold herself responsible if the baby were born deformed. At the same time she acknowledged that she was now seen by the rest of the royal family as "a problem". At formal dinners at Sandringham or Windsor Castle she frequently had to leave the table to be ill. Instead of simply going to bed, she insisted on returning, believing that it was her duty to try and fulfill her obligations.

If daily life was difficult, public duties were

a nightmare. The visit to Wales had been a triumph but Diana had felt overwhelmed by her popularity, the size of the crowds and the proximity of the media. She was riding a tiger and there was no way of escape. For the first few months she trembled at the thought of performing an official engagement on her own. Where possible she would join Charles and remain by his side, silent, attentive but still terrified. When she accepted her first solo public duty, to switch on the Christmas lights at Regent Street in London's West End, she was paralyzed with nerves. She felt sick as she made a brief speech which was delivered in a rapid monotone. At the end of that engagement she was glad to return to Buckingham Palace.

It didn't get any easier. The girl who would only appear in school plays if she had a non-speaking part was now centre stage. It took, by her own admission, six years before she felt comfortable appearing in her starring role. Fortunately for her the camera had already fallen in love with the new royal cover girl. However nervous she may have felt inside, her warm smile and unaffected manner were a photographer's delight. For once the camera did lie, not about the beauty she was becoming but in camouflaging the vulnerable personality behind her effortless capacity to dazzle.

She believes that she was able to smile through the pain thanks to qualities she inherited from her mother. When friends ask how she was able to display such a sunny public countenance she says: "I've got what my mother has got. However bloody you are feeling you can put on the most amazing show of happiness. My mother is an expert at that and I've picked it up. It kept the wolves from the door."

The ability to become this smiling *persona* in public is helped by the nature of bulimia which is a disease where sufferers can maintain their normal body weight — unlike its sister illness, anorexia nervosa where you slim to skin and bone. At the same time Diana's healthy lifestyle of regular exercise, little alcohol and early nights gave her the energy to carry on with her royal duties. As an eating-disorders expert explained: "Bulimics do not admit they have a problem. There are always smiles, no problems in their lives and they spend their time trying to please others. But there is unhappiness underneath because they are frightened to express their anger."

At the same time her deep sense of duty and obligation impelled her to keep up appearances for the sake of the public. A close friend says: "The public side of her was very different from the private side. They wanted a fairy princess to come and touch them and turn everything into gold. All their worries would be forgotten. Little did they realize that the individual was crucifying herself inside." Diana, an unwilling international media celebrity, was having to learn on the hoof. There was no training, backup or advice from within the royal system. Everything was piecemeal and haphazard. Charles's courtiers were used to dealing with a bachelor of fixed habits and a set routine. Marriage changed all that. During the preparations for the wedding there was consternation that Prince Charles would not be able to afford his portion of the expense. "Sums were worked out on the backs of envelopes, it was chaos," recalls one former member of his Household. The momentum which continued long after the wedding took everyone by surprise. Even though extra staff were drafted in, Diana herself sat down to answer many of the 47,000 letters of congratulation and 10,000 gifts which the wedding generated.

She frequently had to pinch herself with the absurdity of it all. One moment she was cleaning floors for a living, the next receiving a pair of brass candlesticks from the King and Queen of Sweden or making small talk with the President of Somewhere or Other. Fortunately her upbringing had given her the social training to cope with these situations. This was just as well because the federal structure of the royal family means that everyone keeps to their own province.

As well as coming to terms with her public role, the fledgling princess had two houses to furnish and decorate. Prince Charles admired her sense of style and colour and left the burden of decoration to her. However, she did need professional help. She welcomed her mother's suggestion of Dudley Poplak, a discreet South African-born interior designer who had furnished her own homes. He set to work on apartments eight and nine at Kensington Palace and Highgrove.

His main task was tastefully to accommodate as many wedding presents into their new homes as was practicable. An eighteenth-century travelling commode from the Duke and Duchess of Wellington, a pair of Georgian chairs from the people of Bermuda and wrought-iron gates from the neighbouring village of Tetbury were just a sample of the cornucopia of presents which had descended on the royal couple.

For much of her pregnancy Diana stayed at Buckingham Palace while painters and carpenters worked at their new London home. It wasn't until five weeks before Prince William was born that the royal couple moved into Kensington Palace, the home also of Princess Margaret, the Duke and Duchess of Gloucester and their immediate neighbours, Prince and Princess Michael of Kent. By then Diana was truly at the end of her tether. She was constantly watched by photographers and reporters while newspapers commented on her every action. Unknown to the Princess, the Queen had already summoned Fleet Street newspaper editors to Buckingham Palace where her press secretary requested that Diana be given a little peace and privacy. The request was ignored.

In February, when Charles and Diana flew to Windermere island in the Bahamas, they were followed by representatives from two tabloid newspapers. The Princess, then five months' pregnant, was photographed running through the surf in a bikini. She and Charles were furious at the publication of the pictures while the palace, reflecting their outrage, remarked that it was one of "the blackest days in British journalism". The honeymoon between the press, the Princess and the palace was effectively over.

This daily media obsession with Diana further burdened her already overstretched mental and physical resources. The bulimia, the morning sickness, her collapsing marriage and her jealousy of Camilla conspired to make her life intolerable. Media interest in the forth-coming birth was just too much to bear. She decided to have the labour induced even though her gynaecologist, George Pinker, has been quoted as saying: "Birth is a natural pro-cess and should be treated as such." While she was well aware of her mother's trauma following the birth of brother John, her in-stincts told her that the baby was well. "It's well cooked," she told a friend before she and Prince Charles travelled to the private Lindo wing of St Mary's Hospital in Paddington, west London.

Her labour was, like her pregnancy, seem-ingly interminable and difficult. Diana was continually sick and at one point Mr Pinker and his fellow doctors considered performing an emergency caesarian operation. During her labour Diana's temperature soared dramati-cally which in turn gave rise to concern for the baby's health. In the end Diana, who had an epidural injection in the base of her spine, was able to give birth thanks to her own ef-forts, without resorting to forceps or an op-eration.

Joy was unconfined. At 9.03 pm on June 21, 1982 Diana produced the son and heir which was cause for national rejoicing. When the Queen came to visit her grandchild the following day her comment was typical. As she looked at the tiny bundle she said drily: "Thank goodness he hasn't got ears like his father." The second in line to the throne was still known officially as "Baby Wales" and it took the couple several days of discussion before they arrived at a name. Prince Charles admitted as much: "We've thought of one or two. There's a bit of an argument about it, but we'll find one eventually." Charles wanted to call his first son "Arthur" and his second "Albert", after Queen Victoria's consort. William and Harry were Diana's choices while her husband's preferences were taken into account in their children's middle names.

When the time came, she was similarly firm about the boys' schooling. Prince Charles argued that they should be brought up initially by Mabel Anderson, his childhood nanny, and then a governess employed to educate the boys for the first few years in the privacy of Kensington Palace. This was the way Prince Charles had been reared and he wanted his boys to follow suit. Diana suggested that her children should go to school with other youngsters. She believes that it is essential that her children grow up in the outside world and not be hidden away in the artificial environment of a royal palace.

Within the confines of the royal schedule Diana has attempted to bring up her children as normally as possible. Her own childhood was evidence enough of the emotional harm which can be wrought when a child is passed from one parental figure to another. She was determined that her children would never be deprived of the cuddles and kisses that she and her brother Charles craved when they were young. While Barbara Barnes, the nanny to Lord and Lady Glenconner's children, was employed it was made clear that Diana would be intimately involved in her children's up-bringing. Initially she breast-fed the boys, a subject she discussed endlessly with her sister Sarah.

For a time the joy of motherhood overcame her eating disorder. Carolyn Bartholomew who visited her at Kensington Palace three days after William was born recalls: "She was thrilled with both herself and the baby. There was a contentment about her." The mood was infectious. For a time Charles surprised his friends by his enthusiasm for the nursery routine. "I was hoping to do some digging," he told Harold Haywood, secretary of the Prince's Trust one Friday evening. "But the ground's so hard that I can't get the spade in. So I expect I'll be nappy changing instead." As William grew, stories filtered out about the Prince joining his son in the bath, of William flushing his shoes down the lavatory or of

Charles cutting short engagements to be with his family.

There were darker tales too: that Diana was suffering from anorexia nervosa; that Prince Charles was concerned about her health; that she was beginning to exert too much influence on his friends and their staff. In reality, the Princess was suffering both from bulimia and a severe case of post-natal depression. The events of the last year had left her mentally drained while she was physically exhausted because of her chronic illness.

The birth of William and the consequent psychological reaction triggered off the black feelings she harboured about her husband's friendship with Camilla Parker-Bowles. There were tears and panic telephone calls when he didn't arrive home on time, nights without sleep when he was away. A friend clearly re-calls the Princess telephoning him in tears. Diana had accidentally overheard her husband talking on a portable telephone while having a bath. She was deeply upset when she heard him say: "Whatever happens I will always love you."

She was weepy and nervy, anxious about her baby — "Is he all right, Barbara?" she would ask her new nanny — while neglecting herself. It was a desperately lonely time. Her family and friends were now at the margins of her new life. At the same time she knew that the royal family perceived her not only as a problem but also as a threat. They were deeply concerned about Prince Charles's decision to give up shooting as well as his inclination towards vegetarianism. As the royal family have large estates in Scotland and Norfolk where hunting, shooting and fishing are an integral part of land management, they were very worried about the future. Diana was blamed for her husband's change of heart. It was a woeful misreading of her position.

Diana felt that she was in no position to influence her husband's behaviour. Changes in his wardrobe were one thing, radical alterations in the traditional country code were quite another. In fact, Charles's highly publicized conversion to vegetarianism can more properly be laid at the door of his former bodyguard, Paul Officer, who frequently argued with him during long car journeys about the virtues of a non-meat diet.

She was also beginning to see the lie of the land with her in-laws. During a ferocious argument with Diana, Charles made clear the royal family's position. He told her in no uncertain terms that his father, the Duke of Edinburgh had agreed that if, after five years, his marriage was not working he could go back to his bachelor ways. Whether those sentiments, uttered in the heat of the moment, are true or not was beside the point. They had the effect of placing Diana on her guard in her every dealing with her in-laws.

At Balmoral her mood grew even more depressed. The weather hardly lifted her spirits. It rained continually and when the Princess was photographed leaving the castle *en route* to London the media jumped to the conclusion that she was bored with the Queen's Highland retreat and wanted to go shopping. In fact, she returned to Kensington Palace for professional treatment for her chronic depression. Over a period of time she was seen by a number of psychotherapists and psychologists who adopted differing approaches to her varied problems. Some suggested drugs, as they had when she was pregnant with William, others tried to explore her psyche.

One of the first to treat her was the noted Jungian psychotherapist Dr Allan McGlashan, a friend of Laurens van der Post, who has consulting rooms conveniently near to Kensington Palace. He was intrigued to analyse her dreams and encouraged her to write them down before he discussed the hidden messages they may have contained. She later told friends that she was not convinced by this form of treatment. As a result he discontinued his visits. However his involvement with the royal family has not ended. Over the last few years he has discussed many confidential matters with Prince Charles who has regularly visited his practice near Sloane Street.

Another doctor, David Mitchell, was more concerned to discuss and analyse Diana's conversations with her husband. He came to see her every evening and asked her to recount the events of that day. She admitted frankly that their dialogues consisted more of tears than words. There were other professional counsellors who saw the Princess. While they had their own ideas and theories, Diana did not feel that any of them came close to understanding the true nature of the turmoil in her heart and mind.

On November 11, Diana's doctor, Michael Linnett, mentioned his concern about her health to her former West Heath pianist, Lily Snipp. She recorded in her diaries: "Diana looked very beautiful and very thin (Her doctor wants her to increase her weight — she has no appetite.) I enquired after Prince William — he slept 13 hours last night! She said that she and Charles are besotted parents and their son is wonderful."

With savage irony, when she was in the depths of despair, the tide of publicity turned against her. She was no longer the fairy-tale Princess but the royal shopaholic who had lavished a fortune on an endless array of new outfits. It was Diana who was held responsible for the steady stream of royal staff who had left their service during the last eighteen months and it was the Princess who was accused of forcing Charles to abandon his friends, change his eating habits and his wardrobe. Even the Queen's press secretary had described their relationship as "rumbustious". At a time when dark thoughts of suicide continually crossed her mind, gossip columnist Nigel Dempster described her as "a fiend and a monster". While it was an appalling parody of the truth, Diana took the criticism very much to heart.

Some time later her brother unwittingly reinforced the impression that she hired and fired staff when he said: "In a quiet way she has weeded out a lot of the hangers-on who surrounded Charles." While he was referring to the Prince's fawning friends, it was interpreted as a comment on the high staff turnover at Kensington Palace and Highgrove.

In reality, Diana was struggling to keep her head above water, let alone undertake a radical management restructuring programme. Yet she shouldered the blame for what the media gleefully called: "Malice at the Palace" describing the Princess as "the mouse that roared". In a moment of exasperation she told

James Whitaker: "I want you to understand that I am not responsible for any sackings. I don't just sack people." Her outburst came following the resignation of Edward Adeane, the Prince's private secretary and a member of the family which had helped to guide the monarchy since the days of George V.

In truth, Diana got on rather well with Adeane, who introduced her to many of the women she accepted as her ladies-in-waiting while she was an enthusiastic matchmaker, continually trying to pair off the difficult bachelor with unattached ladies. When the Prince's devoted valet, Stephen Barry, who later died of AIDS, resigned the blame was laid at Diana's door. She had anticipated as much when he talked to her about leaving as they watched the sun go down over the Mediterranean during the honeymoon cruise. He, like the Prince's detective John McLean and other staff who served the Prince during his bachelorhood, knew it was time to leave once he was married. So it proved.

As she endeavoured to come to terms with the realities of her marriage and royal life, there were moments in those early years when Diana sensed that she actually could cope and could make a positive contribution to the royal family and the wider nation. Those first glimmerings occurred in tragic circumstances.

When Princess Grace of Monaco died in a motor car accident in September 1982, she was determined to attend her funeral. Diana felt a debt of gratitude to the woman who had been so kind to her during that first traumatic public engagement eighteen months before as well as an empathy with someone who, like her, had come into the royal world from the outside. Initially she discussed her desire to go to the funeral with her husband. He was doubtful and told her that she would have to ask the Queen's private secretary for approval. She sent him a memo — the usual form of royal communication — but he replied negatively, arguing that it wasn't possible as she had only been doing the job for a short time. Diana felt so strongly about the issue that, for once, she would not take no for an answer. This time she wrote directly to the Queen who raised no objections to the request. It was her first solo foreign trip representing the royal family and she returned home to praise from the public for her dignified manner at the highly charged and at times mawkish funeral service.

Other challenges were on the horizon. Prince William was still at the crawling stage when they were invited to visit Australia by the government. There was much controversy in the media about how Diana had defied the

164

Queen to take Prince William on her first major overseas visit. In fact it was the Australian Prime Minister, Malcolm Fraser, who was instrumental in this decision. He wrote to the royal couple saying that he appreciated the problems facing a young family and invited them to bring the Prince along as well. Until that moment they were reconciled to leaving him behind for the proposed four-week tour. Fraser's considerate gesture enabled them to lengthen the visit to include a two-week trip to New Zealand. The Queen's permission was never requested.

During the visit William stayed at Woomargama, a 4,000-acre sheep station in New South Wales, with nanny Barbara Barnes and assorted security personnel. While his parents could only be with him during the occasional break in a hectic schedule, at least Diana knew that he was under the same skies. His presence in the country was a useful talking point during their endless walkabouts and Diana in particular delighted in chatting about his progress.

That visit was a test of endurance for Diana. There have been few occasions since then when she has experienced such remorseless enthusiasm. In a country of 17 million people, around one million actually travelled to see them as they journeyed from city to city. At times the welcome bordered on frenzy. In Brisbane where 300,000 people packed together in the city centre, hysteria ran as high as the baking 95 degree temperature. There were many moments when an unexpected surge in the crowd could have resulted in catastrophe. No-one in the royal entourage, including the Prince of Wales, had ever experienced this kind of adulation.

Those first few days were traumatic. She was jet-lagged, anxious and sick with bulimia. After her first engagement at the Alice Springs School of the Air, she and her lady-in-waiting, Anne Beckwith-Smith, consoled each other. Behind closed doors Diana cried her eyes out with nervous exhaustion. She wanted William; she wanted to go home, she wanted to be anywhere but Alice Springs. Even Anne, a mature, practical 29-year-old, was devastated. That first week was an ordeal. She had been thrown in at the deep end and it was a question of sink or swim. Diana drew deeply on her inner resolve and managed to keep going.

While Diana looked to her husband for a lead and guidance, the way the press and public reacted to the royal couple merely served to drive a wedge between them. As in Wales, the crowds complained when Prince Charles went over to their side of the street during a walkabout. Press coverage focused on the

Princess; Charles was confined to a walk-on role. It was the same later that year when they visited Canada for three weeks. As a former member of his Household explained: "He never expected this kind of reaction. After all, he was the Prince of Wales. When he got out of the car people would groan. It hurt his pride and inevitably he became jealous. In the end it was rather like working for two pop stars. It was all very sad and is one reason why now they do everything separately."

In public Charles accepted the revised *status quo* with good grace; in private he blamed Diana. Naturally she pointed out that she never sought this adulation, quite the opposite, and was frankly horrified by media attention. Indeed, for a woman suffering from an illness directly related to self-image, her smiling face on the front cover of every newspaper and magazine did little to help.

Ultimately, the success of that gruelling tour marked a turning point in her royal life. She went out a girl, she returned home a woman. It was nothing like the transformation she would undergo in a few years time but it signalled the slow resurrection of her inner spirit. For a long time she had been out of control, unable to cope with the everyday demands of her new royal role. Now she had developed a self-assurance and experience which allowed her to perform on the public stage. There were still tears and traumas but the worst was over. She gradually started to pick up the threads of her life. For a long time she had not been able to face many of her friends. Confined to a prison, she knew that she would find it unbearable to hear the news from her former circle. In their terms, talk about their holidays, dinner parties and new jobs, seemed mundane compared to her new status as an international superstar. But for Diana this chatter signified freedom, a freedom she could no longer enjoy.

At the same time Diana did not want her friends to see her in such a wretched, unhappy state. She was rather like an injured animal, wanting to lick her wounds in peace and privacy. Following her tours of Australia and Canada she felt enough confidence to renew her friendships and wrote a number of letters asking how everyone was and what they were doing. One was to Adam Russell whom she arranged to meet at an Italian restaurant in Pimlico.

The woman he saw was very different from the happy, mischievous girl he knew from the ski slopes. More confident certainly, but beneath the banter Diana was a very lonely and unhappy young woman. "She was really feeling the bars of the cage chafing. At that time she hadn't come to terms with them," he recalls.

Her greatest luxury in life was to sit down with baked beans on toast and watch television. "That's my idea of paradise," she told him. The most obvious sign of Diana's new life was the sight of her Scotland Yard bodyguard who was seated at a nearby table. It took her a long time to come to terms with that presence; the proximity of an armed police officer was the most potent reminder of the gilded cage she had now entered. It was the little things she missed such as those blissful moments of privacy when she could listen to her favourite composers on the car stereo at full blast. Now she had to consider another person's wishes at all times.

In the early days she would go for an evening "burn up" in her car around central London, leaving her armed Scotland Yard bodyguard behind. On one occasion she was chased through the streets by a car full of excited young Arabs. Nowadays she is more likely to drive to a favourite beach on the south coast so that she can enjoy the wind in her hair and the tang of the sea breeze on her face. She loves being by water, be it the river Dee or the sea. It is the place where she likes to think, to commune with herself.

The presence of a bodyguard was a constant

169

reminder of the invisible veil which separated her from her family and friends. It was the awareness that she was now a possible target for an anonymous terrorist or an unknown madman. The bloody attempt to kidnap Princess Anne on the Mall just yards from Buckingham Palace and the successful break-in to the Queen's bedroom by an unemployed labourer, Michael Fagan, were ample proof of the constant danger the royal family faced. Diana was typically matter of fact in response to this ever-present threat. She went to the headquarters of the Special Air Services in Hereford where she underwent a "terrifying" driving course where she learnt the basic techniques in handling a possible terrorist attack or kidnap attempt. Thunderflashes and smoke bombs were thrown at her car by her "enemies" to make sure that the training was as realistic as possible. On another occasion she went to Lippits Hill in Loughton, Essex, where officers from the Metropolitan Police receive weapons training. There she learnt how to handle a .38 calibre Smith and Wesson revolver and a Hechler and Koch machine pistol which are now standard issue to members of the Royal Protection squad.

She had become reconciled to the idea of an eternal shadow; she discovered that, far from being a threat, her bodyguards were much wiser sounding boards than many of the gentleman courtiers who fluttered around her. Police officers like Sergeant Allan Peters and Inspector Graham Smith became avuncular father figures, defusing tricky situations and deflating overweening subjects alike with a joke or a crisp command. They also brought her mothering instincts to the fore. She remembered their birthdays, sent notes of apology to their wives when they had to accompany her on an overseas tours and ensured that they were "fed and watered" when she went out with them from Kensington Palace. When Graham Smith contracted cancer, she invited him and his wife on holiday to Necker in the Caribbean and also on a Mediterranean cruise on board the yacht owned by Greek tycoon John Latsis. Such is her affection for this popular police officer that she arranged a dinner in his honour after he had recovered which was attended by her family.

If she is dining with friends at San Lorenzo, her favourite restaurant, her current detective, Inspector Ken Wharfe will often join her table at the end of the meal and regale the assembled throng with his jokes. Perhaps she reserves her fondest memories for Sergeant Barry Mannakee who became her bodyguard at a time when she felt lost and alone in the royal world. He sensed her bewilderment and became a shoulder for her to lean on and sometimes to cry on during this painful period. The affectionate bond that built up between them did not go unnoticed either by Prince Charles nor Mannakee's colleagues. Shortly before the wedding of the Duke and Duchess of York in July 1986 he was transferred to other duties, much to Diana's dismay. In the following spring he was tragically killed in a motorcycle accident.

For much of this unhappy early chapter in Diana's royal life, she had excluded those who had been near and dear to her, although Prince Charles still saw his former friends, particularly the Parker-Bowleses and the Palmer-Tomkinsons. The Prince and Princess attended the Parker-Bowleses' house-warming party when they moved from Bolehyde Manor to Middlewich House, twelve miles from Highgrove and Charles regularly saw Camilla when he went fox hunting. At Kensington Palace and Highgrove the couple entertained little, so rarely in fact that their butler Allan Fisher described working for the Waleses as "boring". It was a meagre diet: an annual dinner for Charles's polo playing friends, a "boys only" evening or the occasional lunch with friends like Catherine Soames, Lady Sarah Armstrong-Jones and the then Sarah Ferguson.

The tours, new homes, new baby, and Diana's illnesses took a heavy toll. In her desperation she consulted Penny Thornton, an astrologer introduced to her by Sarah Ferguson. Diana admitted to Penny that she couldn't bear the pressure of her position any longer and that she had to leave the system. "One day you will be allowed out but you will be allowed out as opposed to divorcing," Penny told her, confirming Diana's existing opinion that she would never become queen.

The mood in 1984 was not helped by the fact that she was pregnant with Prince Harry. Once again she suffered badly from morning-sickness although it wasn't as bad as the first time. When she returned from a solo engagement in Norway, Diana was still in the early stages of pregnancy. She and the late Victor Chapman, the Queen's former assistant press secretary, took turns to use the lavatory on the flight home. Characteristically he was suffering from a hangover, she from morning-sickness. It was during those months of waiting that she felt in her heart that her husband was once again seeing Camilla. She felt the signs were there. Late-night telephone calls, unexplained absences and other minor but significant changes in his usual routine. Ironically, during that time, Charles and Diana enjoyed the happiest period of their married life. The balmy summer months before Harry's birth were a time of contentment and mutual devotion. But a storm cloud hovered on the horizon. Diana knew that Charles was desperate for their second child to be a girl. A scan had already shown that her baby was a boy. It was a secret she nursed until the moment he was born at 4.20 pm on Saturday, September 15 in the Lindo wing at St Mary's Hospital. Charles's reaction finally closed the door on any love Diana may have felt for him. "Oh it's a boy," he said, "and he's even got rusty hair." [A common Spencer trait.] With these dismissive remarks he left to play polo. From that moment, as Diana has told friends: "Something inside me died." It was a reaction which marked the beginning of the end of their marriage.

6

"Darling, I'm Going to Disappear"

It was a routine request from the Queen to her daughter-in-law, the Princess of Wales. Royal Ascot race week loomed and she was in the process of drawing up a guest list for the traditional house party at Windsor Castle. Would the Princess like to recommend two single girls of good breeding who would be acceptable guests? She duly put forward the names of two friends, Susie Fenwick and Sarah Ferguson, the daughter of Prince Charles's polo manager Major Ronald Ferguson.

Sarah, a vivacious redhead known by one and all as "Fergie", first met Diana during the early days of her romance with Prince Charles when she watched him play polo at Cowdray Park near the Sussex home of Sarah's mother, Susie Barrantes. Fourth cousins by marriage, the girls had been aware of each other for much longer and had a number of friends in common. They soon became good friends. Sarah was invited to Diana's wedding and entertained her royal friend in her apartment near Clapham Junction in south London.

At one of Sarah's cocktail parties at her home in Lavender Gardens, Diana met Paddy McNally, a motor racing entrepreneur who enjoyed an uneven and ultimately unhappy romance with Fergie. It was Paddy who, on a June day in 1985, dropped Sarah at Windsor Castle's private entrance where she was met by a footman and taken to her room by one of the Queen's ladies-in-waiting. By the side of her bed there was a card, embossed with the Queen's cypher, giving the times of meals and table placements as well as a note saying how the various guests would be conveyed to the racecourse, either in open carriages or black Daimler saloons. Even though her family had rubbed shoulders with the royal family for years, Sarah was understandably nervous. She arrived promptly in the Green Drawing Room for pre-lunch drinks and then found herself seated next to Prince Andrew, who was on leave from his Royal Navy flying duties.

They discovered an instant rapport. He teased her by trying to feed her chocolate profiteroles. She refused, playfully punching his shoulder and claiming one of her interminable diets as an excuse. "There are always humble beginnings; it's got to start somewhere," said Andrew at their engagement interview eight months later. While Diana has been billed as the matchmaker in this royal romance, the truth is that she never noticed the romantic spark between her brother-in-law and one of her best friends. After all, Sarah was involved in a long-term relationship with Paddy McNally while Prince Andrew still had a soft spot for Katherine "Koo" Stark, an American actress who had excited considerable media interest because of her appearance in several soft-porn films.

Diana was favourably impressed when she met Koo during her romance with Andrew. The Princess had known Andrew since childhood and had always been aware that beneath the brash, noisy mask was a much shrewder and lonelier character than he or his family would admit. Charles was only ever jealous of him when he served with some distinction as a helicopter pilot during the Falklands war. While he returned from that campaign with greater maturity, even his best friends would never describe him as a man of great ambition. In his free time he was happy to watch cartoons and videos on TV or aimlessly wander around the various royal apartments, chatting to kitchen staff or watching Diana perform her ballet exercises at Kensington Palace. Diana had seen how Koo Stark, gentle, quiet and utterly devoted, had given this rather lonely man the affection and friendship he was seeking. So when Andrew started seeing

Sarah, the Princess took a back seat. She told her friend: "I'm there if you need me." As their romance developed, Diana was happy to agree to Andrew's requests that he and Sarah stay at Highgrove for the weekend. As Sarah's stepmother, Susan Ferguson said: "Things got better and better between them as the weeks passed by. There was never any 'is it on or is it off?' It wasn't as complicated because they got on so well together. That was the nice thing about it, a straightforward love story. Of course if Sarah hadn't been a friend of the Princess of Wales the situation would have been far more difficult in the early stages. She made it easier for Sarah to see him. You have to remember that in his position it is very difficult to meet women."

As with Diana's romance, events began to take on a momentum of their own. The Queen invited Sarah to stay at Sandringham in January 1986; soon after, Charles and Diana took her skiing to Klosters in Switzerland. Diana loaned Sarah a black and white check coat when they visited Prince Andrew on board his ship, HMS *Brazen,* which was docked in the Port of London. Diana deftly guided Sarah through her first public appearance with members of the royal family. Compared with the aspiring newcomer, Diana seemed the accomplished performer in front of the cameras.

She had blossomed into a sophisticated beauty whose innate sense of style was celebrated the world over.

The traumas of child-bearing, home-making and marriage-building behind her, it seemed to the outsider that Diana had at last come to terms with her royal role. After all, she was still basking in the plaudits following her first television appearance since her engagement. A few weeks earlier she and Prince Charles had been interviewed at Kensington Palace by the veteran newsreader, Sir Alastair Burnet. She was pleased that she had answered his questions clearly and calmly, a fact which did not go unnoticed by other members of the royal family. At the same time High Society was still buzzing about her impromptu performance on the stage of the Royal Opera House, Covent Garden with the ballet star Wayne Sleep. They had secretly choreographed a routine to Billy Joel's song "Uptown Girl" using her drawing-room at Kensington Palace as their rehearsal studio. Prince Charles watched the Gala performance from the royal box oblivious to his wife's plan.

Two numbers before the end she left his side and changed into a silver silk dress before Wayne beckoned her on stage. The audience let out a collective gasp of astonishment as they went through their routine. They took eight curtain calls, Diana even dropping a curtsey to the royal box. In public Prince Charles confessed himself "absolutely amazed" by Diana's display; in private he expressed his strong disapproval of her behaviour. She was undignified, too thin, too showy.

This totally negative attitude was what she had now come to expect. No matter how hard she tried or what she did, every time she struggled to express something of herself, he crushed her spirit. It wore her down. During the wedding preparations for Sarah and Andrew, there was further evidence of his indifference towards her when they flew to Vancouver to open the mammoth Expo exhibition. Before they went, there were further rumblings about her health and what the tabloids liked to call her "pencil slim" physique. It was rumoured that Diana had used the summer break at Balmoral to have an operation on her nose. Her physical appearance had changed so much during the last four years that plastic surgery seemed to be the only credible explanation. But chronic eating-disorders such as bulimia and anorexia do produce physiological changes and this was the case with the Princess. Diana was fortunate that she did not suffer from hair loss, skin complaints or dental problems as a result of starving her body of essential vitamins and minerals.

Discussion about her diet resurfaced when she fainted during a visit to the California stand during the opening of Expo. Throughout her chronic bulimia, Diana had always managed to eat her breakfast. Before this visit she hadn't eaten for days, only nibbling at a Kit Kat chocolate bar during the flight to Canada's Pacific coast. She felt ghastly as they looked round the various stands. Finally, she put her arm on her husband's shoulder, whispered: "Darling, I think I'm going to disappear" and promptly slid down his side. Her lady-in-waiting, Anne Beckwith-Smith, and their deputy private secretary David Roycroft helped her to a private room where she recovered her composure.

When she finally rejoined her husband she found little sympathy. In a mood of irritated exasperation he told her bluntly that if she was going to faint she should have done so in private. When she returned to the penthouse suite they occupied in the Pan Pacific hotel overlooking Vancouver Bay, Diana flopped down and sobbed her eyes out. She was exhausted, hadn't eaten and was distressed by her husband's uncaring attitude. It was what she had come to expect but his disapproving tone still hurt.

While the rest of the party advised that it would be sensible if the Princess missed that night's official dinner and got some sleep, Charles insisted that she must take her place at the top table, arguing that her absence would create an unnecessary sense of drama. By now Diana realized that she needed help for her condition but knew that this was neither the time nor the place to voice those fears. Instead she allowed the doctor accompanying the tour to prescribe medication to help her through the evening. She managed to finish that leg of the visit but when they arrived in Japan Diana seemed pale, distracted and clearly unwell. Her mood was not helped on their return to Kensington Palace when, shortly before the royal wedding, Barry Mannakee was transferred to other duties. He had been the only one within her immediate circle in whom she could confide her worries about being isolated, about her illness and her position as an outsider within the royal family. With his departure, she felt very lonely indeed.

In some ways the arrival of the Duchess of York made her life less bearable. The newly created Duchess bounded into her new role like an overexcited labrador. At her first Balmoral, a holiday experience which leaves Diana drained and dispirited, the Duchess seemed to take it in her stride. She went riding with the Queen, carriage driving with the Duke of Edinburgh and made a point of spending time with the Queen Mother. The Duchess has always had a chameleon personality, readily conforming to the desires of others. She did it when she mixed with the Verbier set: the well-heeled, sophisticated but savagely sarcastic friends of her former lover, Paddy McNally, and she did it now as she adapted to life within the royal family.

Slightly older than Diana but infinitely more experienced in the ways of the world, the Duchess displayed enthusiasm where Diana showed dismay, hearty jollity compared with Diana's droopy silences and boundless energy against the Princess's constant illness. Fergie was an immediate hit inside the family, Diana was still seen as an enigmatic stranger who held herself aloof. When Fergie arrived like a breath of fresh air, Prince Charles was not slow to make the comparison. "Why can't you be more like Fergie?" he asked. It made a change from his usual refrain, which was to compare her to his much beloved grandmother, the Queen Mother, but the message was the same.

Diana was deeply confused. Her face graced the cover of a million magazines and the public sang her praises, yet her husband and his family rarely gave her a word of encouragement, congratulation or advice. Little wonder then that Diana, who at the time had no sense of self-worth or self-esteem, accepted the royal family's view that she should strive to be more like her sister-in-law. This point was reinforced when the Prince and Princess of Wales went to Majorca as guests of King Juan Carlos of Spain at the Marivent Palace. While the public thought Diana had engineered this "bucket and spade holiday" to escape the rigours of Balmoral, the holiday was Prince Charles's idea. There was even ridiculous gossip romantically connecting Diana with Juan Carlos. Actually the King was much closer to Charles than the Princess who found him far too much of a playboy for her tastes. On that first holiday Diana had a miserable time. She was sick for much of the week whereas Charles was fêted by their hosts. Word soon reached the rest of the royal family. Once again Diana was the problem; once again her husband asked: "Why can't you be more like Fergie?"

While the complete absence of support and the atmosphere of disapproval and criticism undermined Diana's self-confidence, the problem was reinforced by society's expectations of the royal family. Essentially, royal men are judged by what they say, royal women by how they look. As she blossomed into a natural beauty, Diana was defined by her appearance, not by her achievements. For a long time Diana accepted the role of the docile helpmate to her crusading, articulate husband. Her astrologer, Felix Lyle, observes: "One of the worst things that happened to her was that she was put on a pedestal which didn't allow her to develop in the direction that she wanted but one which has forced her to be concerned about image and perfection."

Diana was praised for simply existing. For being, not for doing. As one of her informal advisers said: "She was only expected by the royal system to be a clothes horse and an obedient wife. If that is the way you are defined, there is little to praise other than the choice of clothes. If the clothes were partially picked by others then there is nothing to praise. They set her nothing praiseworthy to do." The Duchess of York, this boisterous, independent and energetic young woman, was viewed by Prince Charles, his family and the media as a welcome arrival and a suitable role model for the Princess of Wales. The whole world seemed to encourage Diana to follow her lead.

The first signal of the change in her behaviour was Prince Andrew's stag night when the Princess of Wales and Sarah Ferguson dressed as policewomen in a vain attempt to gatecrash his party. Instead they drank champagne and orange juice at Annabel's night club before returning to Buckingham Palace where they stopped Andrew's car at the entrance as he returned home. Technically the impersonation of police officers is a criminal offence, a point not neglected by several censorious Members of Parliament. For a time this boisterous mood reigned supreme within the royal family. When the Duke and Duchess hosted a party at Windsor Castle as a thank you for everyone who had helped organize their wedding, it was Fergie who encouraged everyone to jump, fully clothed, into the swimming pool. There were numerous noisy dinner parties and a disco in the Waterloo Room at Windsor Castle at Christmas. Fergie even encouraged Diana to join her in an impromptu version of the can-can.

This was but a rehearsal for their first public performance when the girls, accompanied by their husbands, flew to Klosters for a week-long skiing holiday. On the first day they lined up in front of the cameras for the traditional photo-call. For sheer absurdity this annual spectacle takes some beating as ninety assorted photographers laden with ladders and equipment scramble through the snow for positions. Diana and Sarah took this silliness at face value, staging a cabaret on ice as they indulged in a mock conflict, pushing and shoving each other until Prince Charles announced censoriously: "Come on, come on!" Until then Diana's skittish sense of humour had only been seen in flashes, invariably clouded by a mask of blushes and wan silences. So it was a surprised group of photographers who chanced across the Princess in a Klosters cafe that same afternoon. She pointed to the outsize medal on her jacket, joking: "I have awarded it to myself for services to my country because no-one else will." It was an aside which spoke volumes about her underlying self-doubt. The mood of frivolity continued with pillow fights in their chalet at Wolfgang although it would be wrong to characterize the mood on that holiday as a glorified schoolgirls' outing. As one royal guest commented: "It was good fun but within reason. You have to mind your p's and q's when royalty, particularly Prince Charles, is present. It is quite formal and can be rather a strain."

On one occasion Charles, Andrew and Sarah watched a video in the chalet while Diana went out to a local disco where she danced with Peter Greenall, a member of the brewing family, and chatted to old Etonian, Philip Dunne, one of Sarah's childhood friends. Indeed it was the Duchess, who always had a bulging address book even before she entered the royal world, who was asked by Prince Charles to invite two single men along on their holiday. He wanted to make sure that his wife and other female guests, who do not ski as well as he does, had suitable company. The Duchess chose Dunne, a merchant banker who was later described as a "Superman lookalike", and David Waterhouse, then a captain in the Household Cavalry. While the majority of the ski party went on taxing off-piste runs, the two men accompanied Catherine Soames, the former wife of Conservative Member of Parliament Nicholas Soames, and Diana on less exacting slopes. They got along famously. Diana found Waterhouse to be a man of great good humour with a magnetic personality. Philip was "very sweet" but no more. Indeed she was much more friendly with his sister Millie who then worked at Capital Radio running the "Help a London Child" appeal.

Ironically, it was Dunne who became the focus of attention when that summer the unsettled marriage of the Prince and Princess of Wales was examined in some detail. It began with another innocent invitation, this time from Philip's mother, Henrietta, who lives with her husband Thomas Dunne, the Lord Lieutenant of Herefordshire, at Gatley Park. The Dunnes were away for a shooting weekend and so were delighted to offer their home for a house-party. The skiing companions were present as well as a dozen or more other friends. The dozen friends were conveniently forgotten when a gossip columnist mischievously reported that she had stayed alone with Philip Dunne at his parents' home.

The public concern about the marriage of the Prince and Princess of Wales was matched by a growing sense of irritation with the behaviour of younger members of the royal family. The breezy mood of hedonism which everyone enjoyed in the early years of Fergie's royal life was now beginning to grate. Diana was forewarned by her astrologer Penny Thornton. When she visited her in the spring of 1987 she told the Princess that everything she did during the next few months she would pay for.

The skittish behaviour on the ski slopes was followed in April by criticism when Diana was seen giggling as she reviewed the passing-out parade of young army officers at Sandhurst. She subsequently explained that it was the commanding officer's weak jokes as well as her anxiety before making a short speech which caused the nervous laughter. Unfortunately the damage was done and at Royal Ascot two months later she once again came in for critical scrutiny. Photographers captured the moment when Diana and Sarah poked their friend Lulu Blacker in the backside with their rolled umbrellas.

The watching world chorused its disapproval. "Far too much frivolity," sniffed the *Daily Express* while other commentators accused the girls of behaving like actresses in a soap opera. Much was made of Diana's behaviour at the wedding of the Duke of Beaufort's son, the Marquis of Worcester, and the actress Tracy Ward. It was noted that while Prince Charles left early, she danced till the early hours with a number of partners including the gallery owner David Ker, art dealer Gerry Farrell and Philip Dunne. Her dancing style, which was angrily energetic, aroused much comment although little was made of the fact that Charles spent much of the evening locked in conversation with Camilla Parker-Bowles.

The name of Philip Dunne appeared once more when he was wrongly described as her partner at a David Bowie concert at the Wembley stadium. In fact it was David Waterhouse who was photographed talking to her while the man sitting next to her, Viscount Linley, was conveniently cut out of the picture. Diana was in tears when she saw the picture in Monday's papers. She was aware of the media interest in her male friends and so was annoyed with herself for allowing David Waterhouse to sit so near. It was a salutary lesson, compounded by the fact that she got, in her words, "slapped wrists" for wearing a pair of leather trousers at the concert. Once again she was trying to behave like Fergie but courtiers at Buckingham Palace did not feel her apparel was suitable for a future queen.

Worse was to come. On September 22, Prince Charles flew to Balmoral while Diana and the children remained at Kensington Palace. They were not to see each other for well over a month. The strain told. Each time she left Kensington Palace she was conscious that she was being followed by photographers who hoped to capture her at an unguarded moment. She, Julia Samuel and David Waterhouse were snapped as they emerged from a West End cinema. Waterhouse didn't help matters by leaping over a pedestrian barrier and racing off into the night. On another occasion a freelance cameraman claimed he photographed the Princess indulging in some horseplay with David Waterhouse and other friends when she emerged from the mews home of Kate Menzies. At the same time other cameramen were busy in Scotland. Lady Tryon, known as "Kanga" and one of Charles's trusted confidantes from his bachelor days, was photographed by his side. However no-one in the press mentioned the name of his frequent companion, Camilla Parker-

Bowles, who was also among the house guests.

While the public were unaware of her presence, the Princess knew full well that Camilla was spending much time with Prince Charles. A sense of injustice burned deeply inside her. Every time she was spotted with an unattached man, however innocently, it made banner headlines while her husband's relationship with Camilla barely raised an eyebrow. As Philip Dunne, David Waterhouse and later James Gilbey and Captain James Hewitt realized to their cost, meetings with the Princess of Wales produce a high price in unwelcome publicity.

The crisis in the relationship of the Prince and Princess of Wales became a matter of comment not merely for tabloid newspapers but also for serious journals, radio, television and the foreign media. For once the palace took notice of the media storm. Jimmy Savile, who often acts as a high powered go-between in royal circles, offered his services. In October, as speculation about the Waleses' marriage reached fever-pitch, he suggested to the estranged royal couple that it would be an effective public relations exercise if they visited Dyfed in south Wales which had been devastated by flooding. It would, he argued, help to blunt the damaging gossip.

That short trip was not a success. The mood

was set when Diana joined her husband at RAF Northolt for the short flight to Swansea. In a scene witnessed by numerous members of staff, the estrangement between the couple was made plain. Diana was already agitated before she saw her husband but she was unprepared for his hostility as she boarded the BAe 146 jet of the Queen's Flight. When she tried to explain that she had had a terrible time from the media who had followed her every move, the Prince was completely unsympathetic. "Oh God, what is the matter," he said in resigned tones as she talked about the difficulty of performing her public duties in such an atmosphere. He refused to listen and for much of the flight ignored her presence. "It was terrible," she told friends later. "I was crying out for help." The distance in their personal relations was underlined when, at the end of the visit, they returned once more to opposite ends of the country.

It was time for the Princess to take stock. She remembers the occasion well, driving out of the claustrophobia of Kensington Palace with its spy cameras, watchful courtiers and prison walls to her favourite stretch of beach on the Dorset coast. As she walked the lonely sands, Diana realized that any hopes she may have harboured of a reconciliation with her husband were over. His hostile indifference made thoughts of starting afresh completely unrealistic. She had tried to conform to everything he wanted but her efforts at aping the behaviour of the Duchess of York, whom Prince Charles so admired, had been an unmitigated disaster. It brought Charles no closer to her and only served to make a mockery of her public image. The Princess for her own part felt deeply uncomfortable with the world of shallow frivolity epitomized by the Duchess of York. She knew in her heart that in order to survive she had to rediscover the real Diana Spencer, the girl whose character had for seven years been forsaken and submerged. It was time to face the facts of her life. For a long time she had been out of control, meekly agreeing to the wishes of her husband, the royal family and the media. On that long lonely walk she began to accept the challenges of her position and her destiny. Now was the moment to start believing in herself.

7

"My Life Has Changed Its Course"

The Princess of Wales was feeling sorry for herself. Her skiing holiday had been spoiled by a nasty dose of influenza which confined her to bed for days. Early in the afternoon of March 10, 1988, the bedraggled figure of the Duchess of York appeared at her bedside in their secluded rented chalet at Wolfgang near the town of Klosters. Fergie, who was then pregnant with Princess Beatrice, was skiing down the black Christobel run when she took an uncharacteristic tumble and landed ignominiously on her back in a mountain stream.

She was examined by a local doctor and, pale and shaken, driven back to the chalet. As the girls were chatting, they heard a helicopter fly over. They were both filled with foreboding that there had been an avalanche which had somehow affected their skiing party. They were all on tenterhooks when shortly afterwards Prince Charles's press secretary, Philip Mackie, came into the chalet. He didn't know there was anyone upstairs and the girls could hear him saying: "There's been an accident." When he had completed his telephone call they shouted down and asked him what was wrong. Mackie, a former deputy editor of the *Edinburgh Evening News,* tried to shrug off the questions. "We'll tell you soon," he said. For once Diana would not be put off by a palace courtier and was insistent he tell them what was going on. He told them that there had been an accident on the slopes and one of the party was dead.

For what seemed like an eternity the Princess and her sister-in-law sat at the top of the stairs, hardly daring to breath let alone move, as they waited anxiously for more news. Minutes later a call came through to say the victim was a man. Shortly afterwards Prince Charles, sounding shocked and distressed, rang and told Philip Mackie that he was all right but Major Hugh Lindsay, a former equerry to the Queen, had been killed. Everyone started shaking in the first paroxysms of grief. As the Duchess burst into tears, Diana, her stomach churning with emotion, thought it best to deal with practicalities before the full impact of the tragedy overtook them. She packed Hugh's suitcase while Fergie was given his passport to hand to Inspector Tony Parker, Charles's bodyguard. The Princess carefully placed Hugh's signet ring, his watch and his black curly wig which, the night before, he had used for his hilarious Al Jolson impersonation, in the suitcase.

When the suitcase was ready Diana took it downstairs and slid it under Tony Parker's bed so that it would be readily available when they left. The chalet was in uproar that evening with an endless stream of visitors. A Swiss coroner arrived to ask about the circumstances of the accident which occurred when an avalanche overcame the party as they skiied down the Wang, a notorious virtually perpendicular slope which regularly claims lives during the season. Another arrival was Charles Palmer-Tomkinson whose wife Patti was undergoing a seven-hour operation on her legs following injuries she had sustained during the avalanche. Diana was most concerned about Prince Charles's inclination to return to the slopes the following day. The Prince was not immediately convinced that they should abandon their holiday but Diana prevailed. She appreciated that he was suffering from shock and could not at that awful time comprehend the enormity of the tragedy. For once Diana felt absolutely in command of a very trying situation. In fact she was quite bossy, telling her husband that it was their responsibility to return to Britain with Hugh's body. It was, she argued, the least they could do for his wife Sarah, a popular member of the Buckingham

197

Palace press office who had only been married a few months and was expecting her first child.

The next day the party flew back to RAF Northolt outside London where Sarah, then six months pregnant, watched as her husband's coffin was unloaded, with due military ceremony, from the aircraft. As the royal party stood with Sarah, Diana remembers thinking: "You just don't know what you are going to go through in the next few days." Her instincts proved too painfully true. She stayed with Diana and her sister Jane for a few days at Highgrove as she tried to come to terms with Hugh's death. There were tears from dawn till dusk as Sarah and Diana talked about Hugh and what he had meant to her. His loss was all the harder to bear because he had been killed overseas.

The tragedy had a profound effect on Diana. It taught her that not only could she cope with a crisis but that she could also take control and make significant decisions in the face of opposition from her husband. Klosters was the beginning of the slow process of awakening to the qualities and possibilities which lay within herself.

A terse telephone call from her friend Carolyn Bartholomew opened another window into herself. For some time Carolyn had been concerned about Diana's bulimia and had discovered to her horror that chronic deprivation of vital minerals such as chromium, zinc and potassium can lead to depressions and tiredness. She phoned Diana and urged her to see a doctor. Diana didn't have the will to discuss her problems with a specialist. Carolyn issued a sharp ultimatum. She either saw a doctor or she would tell the world about Diana's condition which she had so far managed to keep secret. Diana spoke to the Spencer family's local doctor who recommended her to Dr Maurice Lipsedge, a specialist in eating-disorders who works at Guy's Hospital in central London. From the moment he walked into her drawing-room at Kensington Palace, she sensed that he was an understanding man in whom she could place her trust. He wasted no time with social niceties, asking her immediately how many times she had tried to commit suicide. While she was taken aback by this abrupt question, her reply was equally forthright: "Four or five times."

He fired questions at her for two hours before telling her that he could help her to recover in no time at all. In fact he was confident enough to state categorically that if she managed to keep her food down, in six months time she would be a new person. Dr Lipsedge concluded that the problem did not lie with the Princess but with her husband. For the next few months he visited her every week. He encouraged her to read books about her condition. Even though she had to read them secretly in case they were seen by her husband or members of staff, she found herself inwardly rejoicing as she turned over the pages. "This is me, this is me, I'm not the only one," she told Carolyn.

The doctor's diagnosis bolstered her budding sense of self-esteem. She needed every scrap of help. Even as she started the long haul to recovery, her husband derided her efforts. At mealtimes he would watch her eat and say: "Is that going to reappear later? What a waste." Dr Lipsedge's prediction proved correct. After six months the improvement was noticeable. It felt, she said, as if she had been born again. Before she began her treatment she was regularly sick four times a day. Now this is reduced to once every three weeks. However when she is with the royal family at Balmoral, Sandringham or Windsor, the tensions and pressures trigger a more serious recurrence. The same is true of Highgrove, the couple's country house which she perceives as Charles's territory where he entertains Camilla Parker-Bowles and other members of his set. From the beginning she has disliked the Georgian manor-house and the passage of time has merely exacerbated those feelings. Each weekend she spends there with her husband brings on anxiety followed shortly by an attack of bulimia.

At the same time that she determined finally to conquer her bulimia she decided to confront the woman who had brought such pain, deceit and anger into her life. It happened when she and Prince Charles attended the 40th birthday party of Camilla Parker-Bowles's sister, Annabel Elliot, which was held at Ham Common near Richmond Park. There was an unspoken assumption among the forty guests that Diana would not appear. There was a frisson of surprise among the assembled company when she walked in. After dinner, Diana, who was chatting to guests in an upstairs room, noted the absence of her husband and Camilla Parker-Bowles. She went downstairs and found her husband, Camilla and other guests chatting. The Princess asked the others to leave because she had something important to say to Camilla.

They duly departed and the two women faced each other. Diana told Camilla that she hadn't been born yesterday and that she suspected something was going on between Camilla and Charles. Camilla protested her innocence. At Highgrove Diana routinely pressed the "last number redial" button on his portable telephone. Invariably she was connected to Middlewich House, the Parker-

Bowleses' Wiltshire home. She also resented the regular correspondence between her husband and Mrs Parker-Bowles, especially as they used a go-between to convey their letters. The meetings between Camilla and Charles while out fox-hunting or as guests at Balmoral and Sandringham merely added fuel to her suspicions.

During that confrontation, seven years of pent-up anger, jealousy and frustration came flooding out. The experience resulted in a profound change in Diana's attitude. Although she still felt tremendous resentment towards her husband and Camilla, it was no longer the consuming passion in her life.

It was during this time that she became good friends with Mara and Lorenzo Berni, who run the San Lorenzo restaurant in fashionable Beauchamp Place in Knightsbridge. Mara, who has the reputation of an Italian earth mother, regularly asks guests about their star signs, the meaning of their names and the importance of the planets. While Diana has been visiting the restaurant for some years, Mara and Lorenzo first came properly into her life about three years ago. She was waiting for her lunchtime guest when Mara, who tends to be protective and attentive to favoured guests, wandered over to her table and sat down. Putting her hand on Diana's wrist she told her that she understood what she was going through. Diana was sceptical and asked her to justify her statement. In a few sentences Mara painted a pen portrait of Diana's solitary, sorrowful life, the changes she was undergoing and the path she would take. Diana was transfixed, astonished by her acute observations on the nature of her life which she thought she had managed to disguise from the outside world.

She peppered Mara with questions about her future, if she would find happiness and if she would ever escape from the royal system. From then on, San Lorenzo became much more than a restaurant but a safe haven from her turbulent life at Kensington Palace. Mara and Lorenzo became comforting counsellors who listened as the Princess discussed her many woes. As their friend James Gilbey observes: "Mara and Lorenzo are highly attuned, very perceptive and have seen a lot of unhappiness and frustration in Diana. They have been able to help her come to terms with her situation." The couple encouraged Diana's interest in astrology, tarot cards and other realms of alternative metaphysics such as clairvoyance and hypnotism. It is something of a tradition in the royal family. Author John Dale has traced what he calls the "psychic bloodline of the royal family" back to the days of Queen

Victoria. Over the years, claims Dale, numerous members of the royal family, including the Queen Mother, the Queen and Prince Philip have attended seances and other investigations into the paranormal. Around this time Diana was introduced to the astrologer Debbie Frank who has been consulted by the Princess over the last three years. Hers is a gentle technique which combines general counselling and analysis concerning the present and the future as they relate to the conjunction of planets appropriate to Diana's birth time and date. Born under the sign of Cancer, Diana has many qualities typical of that sign: protective, tenacious, emotionally attuned and nurturing.

When she first began investigating the possibilities of the spiritual world, Diana was very open, almost too open, to belief. She was so much at sea in her world that she clutched at any prediction, in the way that a drowning man clutches at flotsam. As her confidence in herself has grown, particularly over the last few months, she has started to see these methods of self-analysis and forecast as tools and guides rather than a lifeline to grab onto. She finds astrology interesting, occasionally relevant and reassuring, but in no way at all the dominant motivation of her life. As her friend Angela Serota observes: "Learning about the inner growth in ourselves is the most important part of life. This is her next journey."

This interest has been a vital stepping-stone on her road to self-knowledge. Her open-minded approach to philosophies outside mainstream Western thought echoes that expressed by Prince Charles. Just as the Prince and other members of the royal family have allied themselves to alternative medicine and holistic beliefs, so Diana has independently explored alternative methods of approaching the world. Astrology is one such field of inquiry. For most of her adult life Diana had allowed herself to be governed by others, particularly her husband. Consequently her true nature was submerged for so long that it took time for it to resurface. Her voyage of self-discovery was by no means a smooth passage. For every day she felt at peace with herself there were weeks of depression, anxiety and self-doubt. During these black periods the counselling of therapist Stephen Twigg was crucial and the Princess readily acknowledges the debt she owes him. He has been visiting Kensington Palace ostensibly to perform relaxing massage since December 1988. After training in Swedish and deep tissue massage, he evolved a coherent philosophy towards health which, as with Chinese medicine, links the mind and body in the pursuit of well-being.

Her appreciation of Stephen Twigg does not surprise Baroness Falkender, former political secretary to the Labour Prime Minister, Harold Wilson, who has been one of his patients for some time following her illness with breast cancer. She states: "He must have helped her an awful lot as he has helped me. He is a remarkable character. While he is extremely good at therapeutic massage, he has a complete philosophy of life which is challenging and helps you find your own path in life. He makes you feel confident and relaxed and that in turn gives you a new lease of life."

During his consultations with Diana, which last around an hour, he discusses everything from vitamin supplements to the meaning of the universe as he endeavours to enable his patients to understand themselves and bring into harmony their physical, mental and spiritual components. It was at his suggestion that Diana tried vitamin supplements, used detoxifying processes and started to follow the Hay diet which is a system of eating based on keeping carbohydrates and proteins apart in a defined eating pattern. As with all his patients, he discusses processes whereby individuals affirm their positive characteristics and examine threatening situations in their lives — for instance Diana's visits to Balmoral, which made her feel so vulnerable and excluded. "Remember," he told her, "it's not so much that you are stuck with the royal family, rather they are stuck with you."

As Twigg says: "People like Diana show us all that it doesn't matter how much you have or what benefits you are born with, your world can still be restricted by unhappiness and ill health. It still takes courage to recognize these limitations, to confront them and change your life."

She has experimented with other techniques including hypnotherapy with Roderick Lane and aromatherapy, an ancient art which involves the use of aromatic oils to reduce stress, promote physical health and a serenity of mind. "It has a deep relaxing effect," says Sue Beechey, a Yorkshirewoman who has been practising the art for twenty years. She makes up the oils in her Chelsea practice herself before bringing them to Kensington Palace. Diana often combines this with a session of acupuncture, a Chinese healing art in which needles are used to puncture the skin at certain defined points in order to restore the balance of "chi energy" which is essential to good health. The needles stimulate invisible lines of energy called meridians which run beneath the skin. It is performed by Oonagh Toffolo, a trained nurse from County Sligo in Ireland who has been seeing Diana at Kensington Palace for nearly three years and has on occasion treated Prince William. Like Jane Fonda and Shirley MacLaine, the Princess of Wales also has faith in the healing power of crystals.

She keeps physically fit with a daily swim at Buckingham Palace as well as exercise classes and the occasional work out with the London City Ballet of which she is patron. At the same time she has a personal instructor who trains her in the subtle skills of tai chi chuan, a slow-moving meditation popular in the Far East. The movements are graceful and flowing and follow a set pattern, enabling an individual to harmonize mind, body and spirit. Her appreciation is all the more discerning because of her lifelong love of ballet. This gentle physical meditation is matched by the inner peace she finds through quiet meditation and prayer, often with Oonagh Toffolo whose Catholic faith has been tempered by her work in India and the Far East.

While she still reads romantic fiction by authors such as Danielle Steele, who sends her signed copies of her latest books, she is drawn to works dealing with holistic philosophy, healing and mental health. Often in the morning she explores the thinking of the Bulgarian philosopher Mikhail Ivanov. It is a quiet meditation in a crowded day. She cherishes a blue leather bound copy of *The Prophet* by the Lebanese philosopher Kahlil Gibran which was given to her by Adrian Ward-Jackson whom she helped to nurse as he was dying of AIDS.

Her present preoccupations owe little to her husband whose interest in holistic medicine, architecture and philosophy is widely recognized. When he saw her reading a book called *Facing Death* while she was on holiday he asked her bluntly what she was doing wasting her time reading about those issues. These days she is no longer afraid of coming to terms with her own feelings nor confronting the uncomfortable and disturbing emotions of others as they approach death or for that matter seeing humour and joy in situations of intense sorrow. Her love of choral music, "because it touches the depths", is eloquent testimony to her serious reflective spirit. If she were cast away on a desert island her first three choices would be Mozart's Mass in C and the requiems by Fauré and Verdi.

Over the last few years the counselling, the friendships and the holistic therapies she has embraced have enabled her to win back her personality, a character which has been smothered by her husband, the royal system, and the public's expectations towards their fairy-tale princess. The woman behind the mask is not a flighty, skittish young thing nor a vision of saintly perfection. She is, however, a much quieter, introverted and private person than many would like to believe. As Carolyn Bartholomew says: "She has never liked the media although they've been friends to her. Actually she has always been shy of them."

As she has matured over the last three years the physical changes in her have been noticeable. When she asked Sam McKnight to cut her hair in a shorter sportier style it was a public statement of the way she felt she had altered. Her voice, too, is a barometer of the way she has matured. When she speaks of the "dark ages", her tone is flat and soft, almost fading to nothing, as though dredging thoughts from a dim recess of her heart which she only visits with trepidation. When she is feeling "centred", and in charge of herself her voice is lively, colourful and brimming with wry amusement. When Oonagh Toffolo first visited Diana at Kensington Palace in September 1989 she observed that the Princess was timid and would never look her straight in the eye. She says: "Over the last two years she has got in touch with her own nature and has found a new confidence and sense of liberation which she had never known before." Her observation is borne out by others. As one friend who first met Diana in 1989 recalls: "My initial impression was of a very shy and retiring person. She bowed her head low and hardly looked at me when she spoke. Diana emanated such sadness and vulnerability that I just wanted to give her a hug. She has matured enormously since that time. She now has a purpose in life and is no longer the lost soul of that first meeting."

Her willingness to take on challenging and difficult causes such as AIDS is a reflection of her new found confidence. As her interests move into the world of health she finds that she has less time to devote to her portfolio of patronages. It can have awkward results. She recently endured a sticky meeting with executives from a ballet company who made it clear that they would like her to devote more time to their cause. As she said afterwards: "There are more important things in life than ballet, there are people dying in the streets." Last winter she made seven private visits to hostels for the homeless, often accompanied by Cardinal Basil Hume, the head of the Roman Catholic church in England and Wales who is patron of a trust for the homeless. On one trip in January this year she and Cardinal Hume spent nearly two hours with homeless youngsters at a hostel on the south bank of the Thames. Some teenagers, many with drink and drug problems, greeted her presence with aggressively hostile questions, others were simply surprised that she had bothered to see them on a cold Saturday night.

As she was talking, a drunken Scotsman lurched into the room. "Hey, you're gorgeous," he slurred, totally oblivious of whom he was talking to. When he was told about the identity of the Princess, he was unconcerned. "I don't care who she is, she's gorgeous." While Cardinal Hume was deeply embarrassed, Diana found the incident amusing, perfectly at ease among these young people. In spite of these lapses in manners, she feels very comfortable on these occasions, far more so than when she mixes with the royal family and their courtiers. At Royal Ascot last year she attended the race meeting for just two days out of five before undertaking other engagements. In the past she enjoyed Ascot's annual parade of fashion and horseflesh, but she now finds it frivolous. As she says to friends: "I don't like the glamorous occasions any more. I feel uncomfortable with them. I would much rather be doing something useful."

Ironically it was Prince Charles's love of polo which gave Diana a greater understanding of her own worth. The Prince broke his right arm during a game at Cirencester in June 1990. He was taken to a local hospital but, after weeks of rest and recuperation, his arm failed to respond to treatment and a second operation was advised. His friends Charles and Patti Palmer-Tomkinson recommended the University Hospital in Nottingham.

Even though it was a National Health Service hospital, the Prince was duly ensconced in his own ward, which had been newly decorated. He brought along with him, from Kensington Palace, his butler Michael Fawcett and his personal chef. During Diana's visits to see her husband, she spent much time with other patients, particularly in the intensive care unit. She comforted Dean Woodward who was in a coma following a car accident and when he recovered she paid a private visit to his family home. It was a spontaneous gesture but Diana was horrified when news of these secret visits reached a wider audience after the family sold their story to national newspapers.

An incident which meant a great deal to Diana took place in that same hospital away from the cameras, smiling dignitaries and the watchful public. The drama began uneventfully three days earlier in a back yard in Balderton, a village near Newark, when housewife Freda Hickling collapsed with a brain haemorrhage. When Diana first saw her behind the screens in the intensive care unit she was on a life-support system. Her husband Peter sat with his wife, holding her hand.

Diana, who was visiting patients in the hospital, had already been told by the consultant that there was little hope of recovery. She quietly asked Peter if she should join him. For the next two hours she sat holding the hands of Peter and Freda Hickling before the specialist informed Peter that his wife was dead. Diana then joined Peter, his stepson Neil and Neil's girlfriend Sue in a private room. Sue, who was so shocked at seeing Freda Hickling on a life-support machine, did not recognize Diana at first, vaguely thinking she was someone from television. "Just call me Diana," said the Princess. She chatted about everyday matters; the size of the hospital, Prince Charles's arm and asked about Neil's forestry business. Eventually Diana decided that Peter could do with a large gin and asked her detective to find one. When he failed to reappear, the Princess successfully found one herself.

Peter, a 53-year-old former council worker, recalls: "She was trying to keep our spirits up. For somebody who didn't know anything about us she was a real professional at handling people and making quick decisions about them. Diana did a great job to keep Neil calm. By the time we left he was chatting to Diana as though he had known her all his life and gave her a kiss on the cheek as we walked down the steps."

His sentiments are endorsed by his stepson, Neil. He says: "She was a very caring, understanding person, somebody you can rely on. She understood about death and grief."

As Neil and Peter were making the funeral arrangements they were surprised and touched to receive a letter from the Princess on Kensington Palace notepaper. Sent on September 4, 1990, it said:

It was another watershed event for a woman who had for so long believed herself worthless, with little to offer the world other than her sense of style. Her life in the royal family had been directly responsible for creating this confusion. As her friend James Gilbey says: "When she went to Pakistan last year she was amazed that five million people turned out just to see her. Diana has this extraordinary battle going on in her mind. 'How can all these people want to see me? and then I get home in the evening and lead this mouse-like existence.' Nobody says: 'Well done.' She has this incredible dichotomy in her mind. She has this adulation out there and this extraordinary vacant life at home. There is nobody and nothing there in the sense that nobody is saying nice things to her — apart of course from the children. She feels she is in an alien world."

Little things mean so much to Diana. She doesn't seek praise but on public engagements if people thank her for helping, it turns a routine duty into a very special moment. Years ago she never believed the plaudits she received, now she is much more comfortable accepting a kind word and a friendly gesture. If she makes a difference, it makes her day. She has discussed with church leaders, including the Archbishop of Canterbury and several leading bishops, the blossoming of this deep-seated need within herself to help those who are sick and dying. "Anywhere I see suffering, that is where I want to be, doing what I can," she says. Visits to specialist hospitals like Stoke

Mandeville or Great Ormond Street Hospital for Sick Children are not a chore but deeply satisfying. As America's First Lady, Barbara Bush, discovered when she joined the Princess on a visit to an AIDS ward of the Middlesex Hospital in July 1991 there is nothing maudlin about Diana's attitude towards the sick. When a bed-bound patient burst into tears as the Princess was chatting to him, Diana spontaneously put her arms around him and gave him an enormous hug. It was a touching moment which affected the First Lady and others who were present. While she has since spoken of the need to give AIDS sufferers a cuddle, for Diana this moment was a personal achievement. As she held him to her, she was giving in to her own self rather than conforming to her role as a princess.

While her involvement with AIDS counselling has met with some hostility, regularly translated into anonymous hate mail, it is part of her desire to help the forgotten victims in society. Her work with leprosy, drug addiction, the homeless and sexually-abused children has brought her in contact with problems and issues which have no easy solutions. As her friend Angela Serota says: "She took on AIDS because she saw this group of people for whom nothing was being done to help. It is a mistake to think that she is only interested in AIDS and the AIDS question. She cares about sickness and illness."

AIDS is an illness which not only demands skilful and sensitive counselling but also the courage to face the taboos surrounding a disease with no known cure. Diana has embraced the personal and social issues generated by AIDS with candour and compassion. As her brother, Charles, says: "It's been good for her to champion a really difficult cause. Anybody can do your run-of-the-mill charity work but you have to be genuinely caring and able to give a lot of yourself to take on something that other people wouldn't dream of touching." He saw those qualities at first hand when he asked an American friend, who was dying of AIDS, to be one of the godfathers at the christening of his daughter Kitty. The flight from New York left him fatigued and he was understandably nervous to be in the royal presence. "Diana realized straightaway what was wrong," recalls Charles, "and went to him and started talking in a really Christian way. She wanted to know that he was all right and getting through the day. Her concern meant an enormous amount to him."

It was her concern and commitment to a friend which last year involved her in perhaps the most emotional period of her life. For five months she secretly helped to care for Adrian

Ward-Jackson who had discovered that he was suffering from AIDS. It was a time of laughter, joy and much sorrow as Adrian, a prominent figure in the world of art, ballet and opera, gradually succumbed to his illness. A man of great charisma and energy, Adrian initially found it difficult to come to terms with his fate when in the mid-1980s he was diagnosed as HIV positive. His work as deputy chairman of the AIDS Crisis Trust, where he first met the Princess, had made him fully aware of the reality of the disease. Finally he broke the news in 1987 to his great friend Angela Serota, a dancer with the Royal Ballet until a leg injury cut short her career and now prominent in promoting dance and ballet. For much of the time, Angela, a woman of serenity and calm practicality, nursed Adrian, always with the support of her two teenage daughters.

He was well enough to receive a CBE at Buckingham Palace in March 1991 for his work in the arts — he was a governor of the Royal Ballet, chairman of the Contemporary Arts Society and a director of the Theatre Museum Association — and it was at a celebratory lunch held at the Tate Gallery that Angela first met the Princess. In April 1991 Adrian's condition deteriorated and he was confined to his Mayfair apartment where Angela was in almost constant attendance. It was from that time that Diana made regular visits, once even bringing her children, Princes William and Harry. From that time Angela and the Princess began to forge a supportive bond as they cared for their friend. Angela recalls: "I thought she was utterly beautiful in a very profound way. She has an inner spirit which shines forth though there was also a sense of pervasive unhappiness about her. I remember loving the way she never wanted me to be formal."

When Diana brought the boys to see her friends, a reflection of her firmly held belief that her role as mother is to bring them up in a way that equips them for every aspect of life and death, Angela saw in William a boy much older and more sensitive than his years. She recalls: "He had a mature view of illness, a perspective which showed awareness of love and commitment."

At first Angela kept in the background, leaving Diana alone in Adrian's room where they chatted about mutual friends and other aspects of life. Often she brought Angela, whom she calls "Dame A", a gift of flowers or similar token. She recalls: "Adrian loved to hear about her day-to-day work and he loved too the social side of life. She made him laugh but there was always the perfect degree of understanding, care and solicitude. This is the point about her, she is not just a decorative figurehead who floats around on a cloud of perfume." The mood in Mount Street was invariably joyous, that sense of happiness that understands about pain. As Angela says: "I don't see death as sad or depressing. It was a great journey he was going on. The Princess was very much in tune with that spirit. She also loved coming for herself, it was an intense experience. At the same time Adrian was revitalized by the healing quality of her presence." Angela read from a number of works by St Francis of Assisi, Kahlil Gibran and the Bible as well as giving Adrian frequent aromatherapy treatments. A high spot was a telephone call from Mother Teresa of Calcutta who also sent a medallion via Indian friends. At his funeral they passed Diana a letter from Mother Teresa saying how much she was looking forward to meeting her when she visited India. Unfortunately Mother Teresa was ill at that time so the Princess made a special journey to Rome where she was recuperating. Nonetheless that affectionate note meant a great deal to the Princess.

When Diana was unable to visit, she telephoned the apartment to check on her friend's condition. On her 30th birthday she wore a gold bracelet which Adrian had given to her as a sign of their affection and solidarity. Nevertheless, Diana's quiet and longstanding commitment to be with Adrian when he died almost foundered. In August his condition worsened and doctors advised that he should be transferred to a private room at St Mary's Hospital, Paddington where he could be treated more effectively. However Diana had to go on a holiday cruise in the Mediterranean with her family on board a yacht owned by the Greek millionaire John Latsis. Provisional plans were made to fly her from the boat by helicopter to a private plane so that she could be with her friend at the end. Before she left, Diana visited Adrian in his home. "I'll hang on for you," he told her. With those words emblazoned on her heart, she flew to Italy, ticking off the hours until she could return.

As soon as she disembarked from the royal flight jet she drove straight to St Mary's Hospital. Angela recalls: "Suddenly there was a knock on the door. It was Diana. I flung my arms around her and took her into the room to see Adrian. She was still dressed in a T-shirt and sporting a sun tan. It was wonderful for Adrian to see her like that."

She eventually went home to Kensington Palace but returned the following day with all kinds of goodies. Her chef Mervyn Wycherley had packed a large picnic hamper for Angela while Prince William walked into the room almost dwarfed by his present of a large jasmine plant from the Highrove greenhouses. Diana's decision to bring William was carefully calculated. By then Adrian was off all medication and very much at peace with himself. "Diana would not have brought her son if Adrian's appearance had been upsetting," says Angela. On his way home, William asked his mother: "If Adrian starts to die when I'm at school will you tell me so that I can be there."

Once more royal duty called, this time Diana had to join the Queen and the rest of the family during their annual retreat at Balmoral. She left on the strict understanding that she was to be called the moment his condition deteriorated, having previously worked out that it would take her seven hours to drive to London from Scotland.

On Monday August 19 he started to fade. Canon Roger Greenacre had already administered last communion but, in the evening, nurses were so alarmed by Adrian's condition that they woke Angela from a catnap and told her that she had better telephone Diana. The last scheduled evening flight to London had departed so Diana tried to hire a private plane. There were none available. Instead she decided to drive the 600 miles from Balmoral to London with her detective. After driving

223

through the night, the Princess arrived at the hospital at 4 am. She maintained a vigil for hours, holding Adrian's hand and stroking his brow.

A similar watch was maintained throughout Tuesday and Wednesday. "We shared everything," recalls Angela. "In the end it was a very long march." Little wonder then that by Wednesday morning Diana felt drained. She was in the corridor snatching a cat nap when in a room four doors away the alarm bells sounded. A mother who had just had a cardiac operation had a further, fatal seizure. Unfortunately the woman's children and family were in the room at the time. As doctors and nurses dashed around with electronic equipment Diana spent her time comforting the distraught relatives. For them it was the grief of disbelief. One moment their mother was talking, the next she was dead. Diana spent much time with them before they left the hospital. As they said goodbye the eldest son told her: "God has taken our mother but has put an angel in her place."

By Thursday the news had leaked out and a group of photographers waited for her outside the hospital. "People thought Diana only came in at the end," says Angela. "Of course it wasn't like that at all, we shared it all." In the early hours of Thursday, August 23 the end came. When Adrian died, Angela went next door to telephone Diana. Before she could speak Diana said: "I'm on my way." Shortly after she arrived they said the Lord's Prayer together and then Diana left her friends to be alone for one last time. "I don't know of anybody else who would have thought of me first," says Angela. Then the protective side of Diana took over. She made up a bed for her friend, tucked her in and kissed her goodnight.

While she was asleep Diana knew that it would be best if Angela joined her family on holiday in France. She packed her suitase for her and telephoned her husband in Mont-pellier to tell him that Angela was flying out as soon as she awoke. Then Diana walked up-stairs to see the baby ward, the same unit where her own sons were born. She felt that it was important to see life as well as death, to try and balance her profound sense of loss with a feeling of rebirth. In those few months Diana had learned much about herself, reflect-ing the new start she had made in life.

It was all the more satisfying because for once she had not bowed to the royal family's pressure. She knew that she had left Balmoral without first seeking permission from the Queen and in the last days there was insistence that she return promptly. The family felt that a token visit would have sufficed and seemed uneasy about her display of loyalty and devotion which clearly went far beyond the traditional call of duty. Her husband had never shown much regard for her interests and he was less than sympathetic to the amount of time she spent caring for her friend. They failed to appreciate that she had made a commitment to Adrian Ward-Jackson, a commitment she was determined to keep. It mattered not whether he was dying of AIDS, cancer or some other disease, she had given her word to be with him at the end. She was not about to breach his trust. At that critical time she felt that her loyalty to her friends mattered as much as her duty towards the royal family. As she recalled to Angela: "You both need me. It's a strange feeling being wanted for myself. Why me?"

While the Princess was Angela's guardian angel at Adrian's funeral, holding her hand throughout the service, it was at his memorial service where she needed her friend's shoulder to cry on. It didn't happen. They tried hard to sit together for the service but Buckingham Palace courtiers would not allow it. As the service at St Paul's Church in Knightsbridge was a formal occasion, the royal family had to sit in pews on the right, the family and friends of the deceased on the left. In grief, as with so much in Diana's life, the heavy hand of royal protocol prevented the Princess from fulfilling this very private moment in the way she would have wished. During the service Diana's grief was apparent as she mourned the man whose road to death had given her such faith in herself.

The Princess no longer felt that she had to disguise her true feelings from the world. She could be herself rather than hide behind a mask. Those months nurturing Adrian had re-ordered her priorities in life. As she wrote to Angela shortly afterwards: "I reached a depth inside which I never imagined was possible. My outlook on life has changed its course and become more positive and balanced."

8

"I Don't Rattle Their Cages"

The Princess of Wales was enjoying lunch with a friend at San Lorenzo when her conversation was interrupted by her bodyguard. He broke the news that her eldest son, Prince William, had been involved in an accident at his private boarding school. Details were sketchy but it was clear that the Prince had suffered a severe blow to his head while he and a fellow pupil were playing with a golf club in the grounds of Ludgrove school in Berkshire. As she hurried from the restaurant, Prince Charles was driving from Highgrove to the Royal Berkshire hospital in Reading where William was taken for tests.

While Prince William had a CT scan to assess the damage to his head, doctors at the Royal Berkshire advised his parents that it would be sensible to transfer him to the Great Ormond Street Hospital for Sick Children in central London. As the convoy sped along the M4 motorway, Diana travelled with her son in the ambulance while Prince Charles followed behind in his Aston Martin sports car.

While William, who was "chirpy and chatty" during the journey, was prepared for surgery, neuro-surgeon Richard Hayward, the Queen's physician Dr Anthony Dawson, and several other doctors surrounded his parents to explain the position. In numerous conversations they were told that he had suffered a depressed fracture of the skull and required an immediate operation under general anaesthetic. They made it clear that there were potentially serious risks, albeit relatively small, both in the operation itself and the possibility that the Prince could have suffered damage to the brain during the initial accident.

Satisfied in his mind that his son was in safe hands, Prince Charles left the hospital to go to a performance of Puccini's *Tosca* at Covent Garden where he was host to a party of a dozen European Community officials including the environmental commissioner who had flown in from Brussels. Meanwhile Prince William, holding his mother's hand, was wheeled into surgery for the seventy-five minute operation. Diana waited anxiously in a nearby room until Richard Hayward walked in to tell her that her son was fine. It was, she said later, one of the longest hours of her life. As she sat with William in his private room, his father boarded the royal train for an overnight journey to north Yorkshire where he was due to attend an environmental study.

Diana held her son's hand and watched as nurses, who came in every twenty minutes, tested his blood pressure, reflexes and shone a light in his eyes. As had been explained to William's parents, a rapid rise in blood pressure, which can prove fatal, is the most feared side-effect of an operation on a head injury. Hence the regular checks. These were suspended at about 3 am when the fire alarm shattered the night-time silence.

The following morning Diana, tired and overwrought, was deeply concerned about newspaper reports which discussed the chances of William suffering from epilepsy. That was just one of a number of worries. As she discussed the issue with a friend, she observed: "You have to support your children in the bad as well as the good times." She was not alone in that conclusion. As Prince Charles wandered over the Yorkshire Dales on his green mission, a phalanx of psychologists, royal watchers and indignant mothers condemned the Prince for his behaviour. "What kind of dad are you?" asked the headline in *The Sun* newspaper.

His decision to put duty before family may have come as a shock to the general public but it was no surprise to his wife. Indeed she accepted his decision to go to the opera as nothing out of the ordinary. For her it was another example in a continuing pattern rather than an aberration. One friend who spoke to her minutes after William came out of the operating theatre commented: "Had this been an isolated incident it would have been unbelievable. She wasn't surprised. It merely confirmed everything she thought about him and reinforced the feeling that he found it difficult to relate to the children. She got no support at all, no cuddles, no affection, nothing."

A view reinforced by Diana's friend James Gilbey: "Her reaction to William's accident was horror and disbelief. By all accounts it was a narrow escape. She can't understand her husband's behaviour so, as a result, she just blocks it out. Diana thinks: 'I know where my loyalties lie: with my son.' "

When the Prince was made aware of the public's wrath, once again his reaction came as no surprise to his wife: he blamed her. Charles accused her of making an "awful nonsense" about the severity of the injury and affected innocence about the possibility that the future heir to the throne could have suffered brain damage. The Queen, who had been briefed by Prince Charles, was surprised and rather shocked when Diana informed her that while her grandson was on the mend it had not been a cut and dried operation.

Several days after the original accident in June 1991, William was recovering sufficiently well to allow the Princess to fulfill a commitment to visit Marlow Community Hospital. As she was leaving, an old man in the crowd collapsed with an attack of angina. Diana rushed over to help rather than leaving it to others. When the Prince saw the media coverage of her sympathetic actions, he accused Diana of behaving like a martyr. His sour response typified the yawning gulf between them and gave substance to Diana's observations on the media interest in their 10th wedding anniversary the following month. She asked in her matter-of-fact way: "What is there to celebrate?"

The dramatically different manner in which the couple responded to William's injury publicaly underlined what those within their immediate circle have known for some time, the fairy-tale marriage between the Prince of Wales and Lady Diana Spencer is over in all but name. The breakdown of their marriage and the virtual collapse of their professional relationship is a source of sadness to many of their friends. This much discussed union which began with such high hopes has now reached an impasse of mutual recrimination and chilling indifferer ce. The Princess has told friends that spiritually their marriage ended the day Prince Harry was born in 1984. The couple, who have had separate bedrooms at their homes for years, stopped sharing the same sleeping quarters during an official visit to Portugal in 1987. Little wonder then that she found a recent article in the *Tatler* magazine which posed the question: "Is Prince Charles too sexy for his own good" absolutely hilarious because of its unintentional irony.

Such is their mutual antipathy that friends have observed that Diana finds her husband's very presence upsetting and disturbing. He in turn views his wife with indifference tinged with dislike. When a Sunday newspaper reported how the Prince had pointedly ignored her at a concert at Buckingham Palace to celebrate the Queen Mother's 90th birthday, she remarked to friends that she found their surprise rather odd. "He ignores me everywhere and has done for a long time. He just dismisses me." She would, for example, never contemplate making any input into any of his special interests such as architecture, the environment or agriculture. Painful experience tells her that any suggestions would be treated with ill-disguised contempt. "He makes her feel intellectually insecure and inferior and constantly reinforces that message," notes a close friend. When Charles took his wife to see *A Woman of No Importance* when he celebrated his 43rd birthday, the irony was not lost on her friends.

A man of considerable charm and humour, Prince Charles also has the unerring ability to freeze out those who disagree with him. That extends to a trio of private secretaries who contradicted him once too often, numerous other courtiers and staff as well as his wife. Diana's mother experienced his ruthless streak as well as his obdurate nature at Prince Harry's christening. When he complained to her that her daughter had delivered a boy with rusty hair, Mrs Shand Kydd, a woman of fierce integrity, told him firmly that he should be thankful that his second son was born healthy. From that moment the Prince of Wales effectively excluded his mother-in-law from his life. The experience has made her much more sympathetic to her daughter's plight.

This divide between the royal couple is now too wide to paper over for the sake of their public image. On a Thursday before Christmas last year she was due to travel to Plymouth to fulfill a rare joint public engagement. She had been with Prince Edward until midnight at a Mozart concert but the following morning she cancelled the visit saying that she had influenza. Although she did feel ill following the concert, the thought of spending the day with her husband made her even more inclined to spend the day in bed.

The constant tightrope courtiers must walk between the royal couple's public and private life was shown when the Princess of Wales was told about her father's death on March 29, 1992 while she was on a skiing holiday in Lech, Austria. She was prepared to fly home on her own, leaving Prince Charles to stay with their children. When he insisted on returning with her, she made the point that it was a bit late for him to start acting the caring husband. In her grief she did not wish to be part of a palace public relations scheme. For once she dug her heels in. She sat in their hotel room with her husband, his private secretary and press secretary ranged against her. They insisted he return with her for the sake of his public image. She refused. Finally, a telephone call was made to the Queen who was staying at Windsor Castle to arbitrate on this increasingly bitter matter. The Princess bowed to her ruling that they should fly home together. At the airport, they were duly met by the assembled media who reported the fact that the Prince was lending his support at Diana's hour of need. The reality was that as soon as the royal couple arrived at Kensington Palace, Prince Charles immediately went to Highgrove, leaving Diana to grieve alone. Two days later Diana drove to the funeral while Charles flew in by helicopter. The friend to whom Diana related this story commented: "He only flew home with her for the sake of his public image. She felt that at a time when she was grieving the death of her father she could at least be given the opportunity to behave in the way she wanted rather than go through this masquerade."

As a close friend commented: "She seems to dread Charles's appearance. The days when she is happiest is when he is in Scotland. When he is at Kensington Palace she feels absolutely at a loss and like a child again. She loses all the ground she has built up when she is on her own."

The changes in her are physical. Her speech, normally rapid, energetic, coloured and strong, degenerates instantly when he is with her. Diana's voice becomes monosyllabic and flat, suffused with an ineffable weariness. It is the same tone that infects her speech when she talks about her parents' divorce and what she calls "the dark ages", the period in her royal life until the late 1980s when she was emotionally crushed by the royal system.

In his presence she reverts to the girl she was a decade ago. She giggles over nothing, starts biting her nails — a habit she gave up some time ago — and takes on the hunted look of a nervous fawn. The strain in their home when they are together is palpable. As Oonagh Toffolo observes: "It is a different atmosphere at Kensington Palace when he is there. It is tense and she is tense. She doesn't have the freedom she would like when he's around. It is quite sad to see the stagnation there." Another frequent guest simply calls it "The Mad House".

When Prince Charles arrived home from a recent private visit to France she found his presence so oppressive that she literally ran out of Kensington Palace. Diana phoned a friend who was grieving over the death of a loved one. She could sense that her chum was crying and said: "Right, I'm coming over now." As her friend recalls: "She came instantly for me but when she arrived she was visibly unsettled. Diana told me: 'I'm here for you but I'm also here for me. My husband appeared and I just had to fly out and escape.' She was all of a dither."

As far as is practicable they lead separate lives, joining forces only to maintain a facade of unity. These reunions merely give the public a glimpse into their isolated existences. At last year's soccer Cup Final at Wembley they sat next to each other but never exchanged a word or glance during the ninety-minute game. More recently Prince Charles missed his wife's cheek and ended up kissing her neck at the end of a polo match during their tour of India. Even their notepaper which used to have a distinctive intertwined "C and D" has been discarded in favour of individual letter-headings.

When she is at Kensington Palace he will be at Highgrove or Birkhall on the Balmoral estate. At Highgrove she has the large four-poster in the master bedroom; he sleeps in a brass bed which he borrowed from his son, Prince William, because he found its extra width more comfortable after he broke his right arm during a polo match. Even these distant sleeping arrangements have led to marital discord. When Prince William asked for his bed back, his father refused. "Sometimes I don't know who the baby is in this family," commented Diana caustically. The days when she affectionately called him "Hubcap" are long gone. As James Gilbey notes: "Their lives are spent in total isolation. It's not as though they ring each other and have sweet chats each evening and say: 'Darling what have you been doing?' It simply doesn't happen."

During a recent lunch with a close friend who is also the mother of two young children, Diana told of an incident which underlines not only the current state of her relationship with her husband but also the protective nature of her son William. She told her friend that the week that Buckingham Palace decided to announce the separation of the Duke and Duchess of York was understandably a trying time for her. She had lost an amicable companion and was acutely aware that the public spotlight would once again fall on her marriage. Yet her husband seemed unmoved by the furore surrounding the separation. He had spent a week touring various stately homes, gathering material for a book he is writing on gardening. When he returned to Kensington Palace he failed to see why his wife should feel strained and rather depressed. He airily dismissed the departure of the Duchess of York and launched, as usual, into a disapproving appraisal of Diana's public works, especially her visit to see Mother Teresa in Rome. Even their staff, by now used to these altercations, were dismayed by this attitude and felt some sympathy when Diana told her husband that unless he changed his attitude towards her and the job she is doing she would have to reconsider her position. In tears, she went upstairs for a bath. While she was regaining her composure, Prince William pushed a handful of paper tissues underneath the bathroom door. "I hate to see you sad," he said.

She is tormented every day and in every way by the dilemma of her position, continually torn between her sense of duty to the

Queen and nation and her desire to find the happiness she craves. Yet in order to find happiness she must divorce; if she divorces she will inevitably lose the children she lives for and who give her such joy. At the same time she faces rejection by the public who are unaware of the lonely reality of her life and accept her smiling image at face value. It is a cruelly circular argument with endless variations and permutations which she discusses regularly with her friends and counsellors.

Her friends have seen their marriage deteriorate over the last three years to a point where it is a war where no quarter is expected or given. At home the battlegrounds are their children and Charles's relationship with Camilla Parker-Bowles. Officially this skirmishing spills over into their public roles as the Prince and Princess of Wales. She gives him nothing, he offers less. Diana reserves one phrase for their most acerbic confrontations. "Remember I am the mother of your children," she says. That particular shell is exploded during their set piece confrontations about Camilla Parker-Bowles.

Courtiers are regularly caught in the crossfire. When Prince Charles was licking his wounds following the public condemnation of his behaviour when Prince William cracked his skull, his private secretary, Commander

Richard Aylard, attempted to make amends. In a handwritten memo he implored his royal principal to be seen in public with his children more frequently so that he could at least be seen to be behaving as a responsible father. At the conclusion of his missive he heavily underlined in red ink and printed in bold capitals a single word: "TRY".

The ploy worked for a while. Prince Charles was seen taking Prince Harry to Wetherby school and was photographed riding and cycling with his sons on the Sandringham estate. But Richard Aylard's modest public relations success was seen as cynical hypocrisy by the Princess of Wales who knows the daily reality of his involvement with his children.

James Gilbey explains: "She thinks he is a bad father, a selfish father, the children have to tie in with what he's doing. He will never delay, cancel or change anything which he has sorted out for their benefit. It's a reflection of the way he was brought up and it is history repeating itself. That's why she gets so sad when he is photographed riding with the children at Sandringham. When I spoke to her about it she was literally having to contain her anger because she thought the picture would represent the fact that he was a good father whereas she has the real story."

Over-protective in the way that single parent families are, she lavishes William and Harry with love, cuddles and affection. They are a point of stability and sanity in her topsy-turvy world. She loves them unconditionally and absolutely, working with singleness of purpose to ensure that they do not suffer the same kind of childhood she did.

It was Diana who chose their schools, their clothes and plans their outings. She negotiates her public duties around their time-tables. A glance through the pages of her official diary signifies as much: the dates of their school plays, term times, and outings all highlighted in green ink. They come first and foremost in her life. So while Charles will send a servant to Ludgrove school to give William a tray of plums from the Highgrove estate, Diana will make time to cheer him from the touchline when he plays left back for his school soccer team. While Charles's absences are accepted by the boys, there are times naturally when they are keen to see their father. During his convalescence after he had broken his right arm, Charles spent much time in Scotland, much to the dismay of Prince William. Diana communicated his hurt to her husband which resulted in the Prince sending his son hand-written faxes about his activities.

Diana's friendship with Captain James Hewitt, which caused comment in the media, blossomed precisely because he was a popular "uncle" figure to her boys. Hewitt, a keen polo player with the laconic sense of humour and reserve reminiscent of a 1930s' matinée idol, taught William and Harry the finer points of horsemanship during his visits to Highgrove and helped Diana overcome her reluctance to renew her equine skills. He is a man of great charm who provided Diana with amusing and sympathetic companionship at a time when she needed a shoulder to lean on because of her husband's neglect. During their friendship she helped choose some of his clothes and bought him tasteful presents. She visited his family home in Devon on several occasions where she was entertained by his parents while her boys went riding with Captain Hewitt. The Princess found these weekend breaks a relaxing interlude in a hectic life.

While their friendship has waned considerably, for a long time Hewitt was an important figure in Diana's life. The distance which now separates the royal couple is demonstrated by the fact that they have marshalled rival battalions of friends in their support. Thus Diana will air her grievances about her husband to a tightly knit phalanx of friends who include her former flatmate Carolyn Bartholomew, Angela Serota, Catherine Soames, the Duke and Duchess of Devonshire,

Lucia Flecha de Lima, wife of the Brazilian ambassador, her sister Jane, who lives a few yards from Diana's apartment, and Mara and Lorenzo Berni. There are other friends like Julia Samuel, Julia Dodd-Noble, David Waterhouse and the actor Terence Stamp, whom she sees for lunch at his London apartment, who are social friends as opposed to the *confidantes* she sounds out for advice on her eternal dilemma.

On his side Prince Charles counts on Andrew and Camilla Parker-Bowles, who live conveniently near to Highgrove at Middlewich House, Camilla's sister, Annabel, and her husband Simon Elliot, skiing friends Charles and Patti Palmer-Tomkinson, Conservative MP Nicholas Soames, the author and philosopher Laurens van der Post, Susan Hussey, a long-serving lady-in-waiting to the Queen, Lord and Lady Tryon as well as the Dutch couple Hugh and Emilie van Cutsem, who recently bought Anmer Hall near Sandringham.

Diana refers to them dimissively as "The Highgrove Set". They pay court to her husband and lip-service to her, allying themselves completely with his perspective on his marriage, his children and his royal life. As a result, friendships have foundered as relations between the Prince and Princess have degenerated. Diana once described Emilie van Cutsem, a former champion golfer, as her best friend. It was she who first informed Lady Diana Spencer of Prince Charles's relationship with Camilla Parker-Bowles. Inevitably suspicion is rife. When the van Cutsems hosted a dinner for Prince Charles and his circle at a Covent Garden restaurant just before Christmas last year the Princess strongly suspected that the date was chosen because she had a long-standing previous engagement and would be unable to attend.

The week of the Princess of Wales's 30th birthday provided graphic evidence of the way their friends have become involved in the rivalry between the royal couple. On the day that a national opinion poll revealed that Diana was the most popular member of the royal family, she received a public slap in the face when a front page story in the *Daily Mail* revealed that the Princess had turned down her husband's offer of a birthday party at Highgrove. The clear implication, illustrated by quotes from the Prince's friends, was that Diana was behaving in an unreasonable manner. When Prince Charles first suggested the idea of a party, the Gulf War was in full flow. Diana believed strongly that planning such a party would be frivolous at a time when British troops were involved in the fighting. Also, as her friends are aware, a party at Highgrove comprising many of Charles's cronies was hardly her idea of fun.

The clear implication of the newspaper article was that Prince Charles had complained about his wife to friends who had decided to take action on his behalf. While her husband protested his innocence, it cast a shadow over her birthday, which she celebrated quietly with her sister Jane and their children. It marked a significant private corrosion of the relations between the royal couple.

The resulting adverse publicity forced a temporary public *rapprochement* upon the couple. Prince Charles altered his diary so that he could appear with his wife at various public engagements, including a concert at the Royal Albert Hall, as well as deciding to spend at least part of their 10th wedding anniversary together to placate the media. It was highly contrived and lasted only a matter of weeks before the truce was breached. Their total separation, epitomized by the presence of the hostile Highgrove Set, is virtually formalized. But Charles's friends are not the only reason why she loathes her country home. She refers to her trips to their Gloucestershire home as "a return to prison" and rarely invites her family or friends. Diana sees it as the place where another woman effectively holds court. Camilla Parker-Bowles acts as hostess to dinners attended by Charles's close friends, choosing everything from the menus to the place settings. As Diana's friend James Gilbey says: "She dislikes Highgrove. She feels that Camilla lives just down the road and regardless of any effort she puts into the house, she never feels it is her home."

Diana took some small satisfaction when a Sunday newspaper accurately detailed Camilla's comings and goings, even reporting on the unmarked Ford estate car the Prince uses to drive the twelve miles to Middlewich House. This was further authenticated by a former policeman at Highgrove, Andrew Jacques, who sold his story to a national newspaper. "Mrs Parker-Bowles certainly figures larger in the Prince's life at Highgrove than Princess Di," he claimed, a view endorsed by many of Diana's friends.

So who is the woman who excites Diana's feelings? From the moment photographs of Camilla fluttered from Prince Charles's diary during their honeymoon to the present day, the Princess of Wales has understandably harboured every kind of suspicion, resentment and jealousy about the woman Charles loved and lost during his bachelor days. Camilla is from sturdy county stock with numerous roots in the aristocracy. She is the daughter of Major

Bruce Shand, a well-to-do wine merchant, Master of Fox Hounds and the Vice Lord Lieutenant of East Sussex. Her brother is the adventurer and author Mark Shand, who was once an escort of Bianca Jagger and model Marie Helvin, and is now married to Clio Goldsmith, niece of the grocery millionaire. Camilla is related to Lady Elspeth Howe, wife of the former Chancellor of the Exchequer, and the millionaire builder, Lord Ashcombe. Her great-grandmother was Alice Keppel who for many years was the mistress of another Prince of Wales, Edward VII. She was married to a serving Army officer and once said that her job was to "curtsey first — and then leap into bed."

In his bachelor days Andrew Parker-Bowles, who is related to the Earls of Derby and Cadogan and the Duke of Marlborough, was a dashing and popular escort among society debutantes. Before his marriage at the Guards Chapel in July 1973, the charming cavalry officer was a companion for Princess Anne and Sir Winston Churchill's granddaughter, Charlotte. He is now a brigadier and the director of the Royal Army Veterinary Corps as well as holder of the improbable title "Silver Stick in Waiting to the Queen". It was in this capacity that he organized the celebration parade along the Mall to mark the Queen

Mother's 90th birthday.

Charles first met Camilla in 1972 while he was serving in the Navy and she was dating his polo friend, Andrew Parker-Bowles, then a captain in the Household Cavalry. He was immediately smitten by this vivacious, attractive young woman who shared his passion for hunting and polo. According to the Prince's biographer, Penny Junor, he fell deeply in love with Camilla. "She was in love with him and would have married him at the drop of a hat. Alas, he never asked her. He dithered and hedged his bets, and could not resist the charms of other women, until Camilla gave up on him. It was only when she was irretrievably gone that the Prince realized what he had lost."

Now 43 and the mother of two teenage children — Prince Charles is godfather to her eldest son Tom — Camilla is seen, in the public mind, in the position of trusted royal *confidante*. In Diana's mind there is no doubt that she is one of the root causes of her failed marriage.

Diana has frequently discussed her concerns about Camilla with her friend James Gilbey. He has provided a sympathetic ear as Diana poured out her feelings of anger and anguish about Camilla. He believes that she is unable to put out of her mind the one-time relationship Camilla enjoyed with Prince Charles. He says: "As a result their marriage is a charade. The whole prospect of Camilla drives her spare. I can understand it. I mean what the hell is that woman doing in her house? This is what she sees as the gross injustice of the thing."

Gilbey, a motor-trade executive, has known Diana since she was 17 but became much closer to her when they met at a party hosted by Julia Samuel. They talked long into the night about their respective love lives — he about a failed romance, she about her fading marriage. In the summer of 1989 she was concerned about winning her husband back and forcing him to make a break with the Highgrove set. He recalls: "There was enormous pride at stake. Her sense of rejection, by her husband and the royal system, was apparent."

At that time she was under pressure from her own family and the royal family to try and make a new start. Diana even agreed that another baby may provide a solution to the problem. However her olive branch was met with the negative indifference which now characterizes their relations. At times the waves of anger, frustration, wounded pride and sense of rejection threatened to overwhelm her. When Prince Charles was convalescing from his broken right arm following a polo accident in 1990, he spent his days at Highgrove or Balmoral where Camilla Parker-Bowles was a regular visitor. Diana stayed at Kensington Palace, unwanted, unloved and humiliated. She unburdened her feelings to Gilbey: "James, I'm just so fed up with it. If I let it get to me I will just upset myself more. So the thing to do is to involve myself in my work; get out and about. If I stop to think I'll go mad."

As a mutual friend, who has watched the royal couple's gradual estrangement, notes: "You can't blame Diana for the anger she must feel given the fact that her husband appears to have this long-standing friendship with another woman. The marriage has deteriorated too much to want to win him back. It's just too late."

Over the last two years, Diana's renewed self-confidence, her changed priorities combined with skilful counselling has blunted the anger she feels towards Camilla. As her marriage has crumbled, she has begun to see Camilla as a less threatening figure and more of a useful means of keeping her husband out of her life. Nonetheless, there are times when she still finds her husband's indifference deeply wounding. When Camilla and her husband joined Prince Charles on a holiday in Turkey shortly before his polo accident, she didn't complain just as she bore, through gritted teeth, Camilla's regular invitations to Balmoral and Sandringham. When Charles flew to Italy last year on a sketching holiday, Diana's friends noted that Camilla was staying at another villa a short drive away. On her return Mrs Parker-Bowles made it quite clear that any suggestion of impropriety was absurd. Her protestations of innocence brought a tight smile from the Princess. That changed to scarcely controlled anger during their summer holiday on board a Greek tycoon's yacht. She quietly simmered as she heard her husband holding forth to dinner-party guests about the virtues of mistresses. Her mood was scarcely helped when, later that evening, she heard him chatting on the telephone to Camilla.

They meet socially on occasion but, there is no love lost between these two women locked into an eternal triangle of rivalry. Diana calls her rival "the rotweiller" while Camilla refers to the Princess as that "ridiculous creature". At social engagements they are at pains to avoid each other. Diana has developed a technique in public of locating Camilla as quickly as possible and then, depending on her mood, she watches Charles when he looks in her direction or simply evades her gaze. "It is a morbid game," says a friend. Days before the Salisbury Cathedral spire appeal concert Diana knew that Camilla was going. She vented her frustration in conversations with friends so that on the day of the event the Princess was able to watch the eye contact between her husband and Camilla with quiet amusement.

Last December all those years of pent-up emotion came flooding out at a memorial service for Leonora Knatchbull, the six-year-old daughter of Lord and Lady Romsey, who tragically died of cancer. As Diana left the service, held at St James's Palace, she was photographed in tears. She was weeping in sorrow but also in anger. Diana was upset that Camilla Parker-Bowles who had only known the Romseys for a short time was also present at such an intimate family service. It was a point she made vigorously to her husband as they travelled back to Kensington Palace in their chauffeur-driven limousine. When they arrived at Kensington Palace the Princess felt so distressed that she ignored the staff Christmas party, which was then in full swing, and went to her sitting-room to recover her composure. Diplomatically, Peter Westmacott, the Waleses' deputy private secretary, sent her avuncular detective Ken Wharfe to help calm her.

The incident at the memorial service

brought to the surface her resentment at her treatment by the royal system and the charade of life at Kensington Palace. Shortly afterwards she vented that anger and frustration when she spoke to a close friend. She made clear that her sense of duty impelled her to fulfill her obligations as the Princess of Wales yet her difficult private life lead her seriously to consider leaving the royal family.

Amid the wreckage of their relationship there are still friends who feel that the rage and jealousy Diana feels towards her husband is reflection of her innermost desire to win him back. Those observers are in a minority. Most are deeply pessimistic about the future. Oonagh Toffolo notes: "I had great hopes until a year ago, now I have no hope at all. It would need a miracle. It is a great pity that these two people with so much to give to the world can't give it together."

A similar conclusion has been reached by a friend, who has discussed Diana's troubles with her at length. She says: "If he had done the work in the early days and forgotten about Camilla, they would have so much more going for them. However they have now reached a point of no return."

The words "there is no hope" are often repeated when friends talk about the Waleses' life together. As one of her closest friends says:

"She has conquered all the challenges presented to her within the profession and got her public life down to a fine art. But the central issue is that she is not fulfilled as a woman because she doesn't have a relationship with her husband." The continual conflict and suspicion in their private life inevitably colours their public work. Nominally the Prince and Princess are a partnership, in reality they act independently, rather like the managing directors of rival companies. As one former member of the Waleses' Household said: "You very quickly learn to choose whose side you are on — his or hers. There is no middle course. There is a magic line that courtiers can cross once or twice. Cross it too often and you are out. That is not a basis for a stable career."

Similar sentiments are expressed by the small army of executives who have passed through Kensington Palace. In February this year David Archibald, Prince Charles's financial director, known as the comptroller, abruptly resigned. The reasons, he told friends, were the difficulties of working in an atmosphere of mutual distrust and jealousy between the two antagonistic offices. As ever the Prince of Wales, who has been described as "Britain's worst boss", blamed the departure on his wife. Archibald had good reason to throw in the towel. These days the rivalry between Charles and Diana ranges from the petty to the pathetic. The first public sign was when both made important speeches, Charles about education, Diana about AIDS, on the same day. One inevitably stole the thunder from the other. That behaviour is part of a continuing cycle. When the couple returned from a joint visit to Canada last year, the Princess wrote a number of thank-you letters to the various charities and government organizations who had arranged the trip. When they were passed to her husband to "top and tail" with his own sentiments he went through each letter and crossed out every reference to "we" and inserted "I" before he was prepared to sign them.

This is not an unusual occurrence. In January 1992, when the Prince sent a bouquet of flowers to Mother Teresa of Calcutta, who was recovering from a heart condition, he ordered his private secretary Richard Aylard to make sure they were sent only from him, not jointly. It mattered little. Diana arranged a special meeting where she flew to the hospital in Rome to see the woman she so admires. Again, during a planning meeting for their joint visit to India in February this year, it was felt that Diana should concentrate on promoting family planning issues. "I think we will change your profile from AIDS to family planning," remarked a diplomat who was impressed by her performance in Pakistan. When Prince Charles was asked about the idea he complained that he wanted to spearhead that particular issue. For once Diana told staff to ignore "the spoiled boy". As one of her closest friends says: "It's time he started seeing her as an asset, not as a threat, and accepted her as an equal partner. At the moment her position within the organization is a very lonely one."

Consultation between the couple is invariably adversarial, taking place within an atmosphere of mutual recrimination. It is so unusual to have a calm discussion about problems that when the Prince approached Diana to consider a confidential report about staff abuses of the royal name, prepared by a senior courtier, the Princess, used to curt indifference, was genuinely surprised. There was concern that the royal name and royal notepaper were being used to acquire clothes discounts, theatre tickets and other perks. While the issue required delicate handling, the most surprising aspect of the episode was the liaison between the Prince and Princess.

While their normal working relations are pervaded by an atmosphere of intrigue and competitive resentment, Diana still feels a sense of responsibility towards her husband. When he returned to public duties last year following a lengthy recuperation from his broken arm he intended to make a bizarre "statement" regarding the intense speculation surrounding his injury. He instructed his staff to find a false arm with a hook on the end so that he could appear in public like a real-life Captain Hook. Diana was consulted by senior courtiers worried that he would make a fool of himself. She suggested that a false arm should be obtained but then conveniently mislaid shortly before he was to attend a medical meeting in Harley Street, central London. While Charles was annoyed by the subterfuge, his staff were relieved that his dignity had been preserved thanks to Diana's timely intervention.

It would be a mistake to assume that the contest between the Prince and Princess of Wales is fought on even terms. The Princess may be the bigger draw to the press and the public but inside the palace walls she is reliant upon revenues from the Duchy of Cornwall, controlled by her husband, to fund her private office while her junior status within the royal hierarchy means that Prince Charles always has the final say. Everything from her attendance at his planning meetings, the composition of joint overseas tours and the office structure is ultimately decided by the Prince of Wales. When she suggested she start a "Princess of Wales Trust" to raise money for her various charities he refused to countenance the idea, knowing that it would take away kudos and cash from his own Prince's Trust charity.

During the Gulf crisis the Princess and her sister-in-law, the Princess Royal, independently came up with the idea of visiting British troops stationed in the Saudi Arabian theatre of operations. They planned to fly out together and were rather looking forward to driving round the desert in tanks and meeting the boys in khaki. However the Queen's private secretary, Sir Robert Fellowes, intervened. The scheme was shelved as it was thought that it would be more appropriate if a more senior royal represented the family. So Prince Charles flew to the Gulf while the Princess of Wales was assigned the supporting task of travelling to Germany to meet the wives and families of troops.

The constant needle and edge in their working relationship is matched by a cloak of secrecy the warring offices throw around their rival operations. Diana had to use all her guile to tease out information from her husband's office before she flew to Pakistan on her first major solo overseas tour last year. She was due to stopover in Oman where Prince Charles was trying to woo the Sultan to win funding for an architectural college. Curious by nature, Diana wanted to know more but realized that a direct approach to Prince Charles or his senior advisers would receive a dusty response. Instead she penned a short memo to the Prince's private secretary, Commander Richard Aylard, and asked innocently if there was anything in the way of briefing notes she needed for the short stopover in Oman. The result was that, as she was travelling on official Foreign Office business, the Prince was forced to reveal his hand.

In this milieu of sullen suspicion, secrecy is a necessary and constant companion. Caution is her watchword. There are plenty of eyes and ears as well as police video cameras to catch the sound of a voice raised in anger or the sight of an unfamiliar visitor. Tongues wag and stories circulate with electrifying efficiency. It is why, when she was learning about her bulimic condition, she hid books on the subject from prying eyes. She dare not bring home tapes from her astrology readings nor read the satirical magazine *Private Eye* with its wickedly accurate portrayal of her husband in case it attracts unfavourable comment. The telephone is her lifeline, spending hours chatting to friends: "Sorry about the noise, I was trying to get my tiara on," she told one disconcerted friend.

She is a hostage to fortune, held captive by her public image, bound by the constitutional circumstance of her unique position as the Princess of Wales and a prisoner of her day to day life. Her friends refer to the acronym POW as meaning "prisoner of war". Indeed the cloying claustrophobia of royal life merely serves to exacerbate her genuine fear of confined spaces. It was brought home to her last year when she went to the National Hospital for a body scan because her doctors feared she may have a cervical rib, a benign growth that often traps nerves below the shoulder blade. Like many patients, once she was inside the enclosed scanning machine, she felt very panicky and needed to be calmed down with a tranquilizer. It meant that an operation which should have lasted 15 minutes took two hours.

She now sends scented candles rather than letters of thanks to those who supply goods and services in case her well-meaning notes get into the wrong hands. Again, before she went skiing in Austria this year with her children and her friends Catherine Soames and David Linley, she agonized over inviting Major David Waterhouse. She had comforted him at his mother's funeral in January and felt a holiday would help ease the loss he felt over her death. However Diana, who has been seen regularly in his company, worried that the wrong interpretation would be placed on his presence and his own life would come under undue scrutiny as a result. He was not invited. Although her children give her immense joy, she also knows that they are her passport to the outside world. She can take them to the theatre, cinema and parks without exciting adverse comment from the media. It does have its drawbacks however. When she took Prince Harry and a party of friends to see Jason Donovan in the musical *Joseph and the Amazing Technicolor Dreamcoat* the Princess had to lurk outside the gentlemen's lavatory during the interval waiting for her charges.

She has to conduct her social life with caution. While her husband has been able to conduct his private life unnoticed for years, Diana is keenly and resentfully aware that every time she is seen with an unattached male, however innocently, it makes headlines. It happened when she visited James Gilbey for dinner at his Knightsbridge apartment as it did when she spent the weekend at the country home of Philip Dunne's parents. There is no respite. She recently had to cancel a lunch date with her friend Terence Stamp because she was made aware that his apartment in the Albany was being "staked out" by newspaper photographers.

Diana's enemies within are the courtiers who watch and judge her every move. If Diana is the current star of the Windsor roadshow then senior courtiers are the producers who hover in the background waiting to criticize her every slip. When she spent three days with her mother in Italy she was driven everywhere by Antonio Pezzo, a handsome member of the family who were her hosts. As she said goodbye she impulsively kissed him on the cheek. She was carpeted for that gesture just as she was ticked-off for praising the way Prime Minister John Major behaved during the Gulf crisis. It was a human reaction to his difficult position as a novice Prime Minister but the Queen's private secretary, Sir Robert Fellowes, felt it sufficiently political to be worthy of unfavourable comment.

The smallest breach of royal behaviour is deserving of complaint. After a film premiere, she attended a party where she enjoyed a long conversation with Liza Minnelli. The following morning it was pointed out that it was not done to attend these occasions. It had a happy result however. She enjoyed a rapport with the Hollywood star who talked at length about her difficult life and told her simply that when she felt down she thought of Diana and that helped her endure. It was a touching and very honest conversation between two women who have suffered much in life and has since formed the basis of a long-distance friendship.

It is little wonder then that the Princess, trusting by nature, trusts very few in the royal organization. She opens her own mail when she returns from her morning swim at Buckingham Palace so that she can see at first hand what the general public are thinking. It means that she does not have to rely on the cautious filter of her staff. This policy has yielded several satisfying side effects. A letter from a father whose son was dying of AIDS particularly touched her. Before he died, the young man's last request was to meet the Princess of Wales. His father wrote to Diana in June last year but with little hope of success. After reading his plea, Diana personally arranged for his son to attend an AIDS hostel in London run by the Lighthouse Trust which she was scheduled to visit. Her thoughtful gesture made his dying wish come true. If the letter had been processed in the usual way the family would probably have received a sympathetic but noncommittal reply from a lady-in-waiting.

Such is her lack of confidence in these traditional royal helpmates, whose duties are to accompany her on public engagements and undertake administrative tasks, that they are gradually being phased out. She has recently taken to employing her elder sister Sarah in this capacity — she travelled with her to Budapest in Hungary on an official visit in March, 1992 — or goes on what she calls her "away-days" on her own. As one friend remarks: "She had these terrific run-ins with her ladies-in-waiting, particularly Anne Beckwith-Smith (her one-time private secretary). She felt they were holding her back, being too protective and too 'in' with the system."

Instead she prefers to consult those who are tangential to the system. From time to time she will phone Major-General Sir Christopher Airey at his Devon home for advice. Airey, who was abruptly dismissed as Prince Charles's private secretary last year, is sufficiently aware of the machinations within the system to guide her sensibly. For a time Jimmy Savile helped smooth her public image while Terence Stamp gave her general guidance on her speech-making. She also relies on a coterie of unofficial counsellors, who prefer to remain anonymous, to sound out ideas and problems. They polish her speeches, advise on ticklish staff problems and give fair warning of possible publicity difficulties.

She is attracted to outsiders precisely because she feels so alienated from the royal system. As James Gilbey says: "She gets on much better with them than the men in grey because they are tied up with preserving a system which she feels is outdated. There is a natural built-in confrontation there. They are trying to uphold something and she is trying to get out." Her astrologer Felix Lyle observes: "She has a soaring spirit and optimism which is easily defeated. Dominated by those with strong character, she does not yet have enough self-confidence to take on the system."

It is a view endorsed by another friend who says: "The whole royal business terrified her. They gave her no confidence or support." As her confidence has developed she now believes that she cannot achieve her true potential within the current royal restraints. She tells friends: "Inside the system I was treated very differently, as though I was an oddball. I felt I wasn't good enough. Now, thank God, I think it's okay to be different."

Diana has led a confusing double life where she is celebrated by the public but watched in doubtful and often jealous silence by her husband and the rest of his family. The world judges that she has dusted off the dowdy image of the House of Windsor but within the royal family, reared on values of control, distance and formality, she is seen as an outsider and a problem. She is tactile, emotional, gently irreverent and spontaneous. For a white-gloved, stiff-upper-lip institution with a large "Do not touch" sign hanging from its crown, the Princess of Wales is a threat. Experience has taught her not to trust or confide in members of the royal family. As with Prince Philip's advice to his son about Camilla Parker-Bowles, she realizes that blood ties matter most. As a result she has kept a deliberate distance from her in-laws, skirting round issues, avoiding confrontations and locking herself away in her ivory tower. It has been a double-edged sword as she has failed to build any bridges, so essential in a closed world infected by family and office politics. She has few allies within the royal family. "I don't rattle their cages and they don't rattle mine," she says.

So while she loves Scotland and grew up in Norfolk, she finds the atmosphere at Balmoral and Sandringham totally draining of her spirit and vitality. It is during these family holidays where her bulimia is at its worst and where she will try any ploy to escape for a few days. Diana lives the reality behind the public impression of unshakeable unity the monarchy exudes. She knows that in private the contemporary Court is not so very different from previous reigns in its squabbling, feuds, and in-fighting.

At the heart of the royal family is the tightly-knit and implacable troika of the Queen Mother and her daughters, the Queen and Princess Margaret. As author Douglas Keay perceptively observes in his profile of the Queen: "Cross one and you cross them all." Diana's relations with these three central characters are uneven. She has much time for Princess Margaret, a neighbour at Kensington Palace, whom she acknowledges as giving her the most help in acclimatizing herself to the rarified royal world. "I've always adored Margo," she says. "I love her to bits and she's been wonderful to me from day one."

It is much less cordial with the Queen Mother. Diana sees her London home, Clarence House, as the font of all negative comment about herself and her mother. She keeps a distrustful distance from this matriarchal figure, describing social occasions hosted by the Queen Mother as stiff and overly formal. It was, after all, Diana's grandmother, the Queen Mother's lady-in-waiting, who testified in court about her daughter's unsuitability to look after her four children. Her view was accepted by the judge and the hostility and bitterness within the divided Spencer family is still sharp. At the same time the Queen Mother, unfavourably predisposed to Diana and her mother, exercises an enormous influence over the Prince of Wales. It is a mutual adoration society from which Diana is effectively excluded. "The Queen Mother drives a wedge between Diana and the others," notes a friend. "As a result she makes every excuse to avoid her."

Diana's relationship with the Queen is much friendlier. However it is governed by the fact that she is married to her eldest son and the future monarch. In the early days Diana was quite simply terrified of her mother-in-law. She kept to the formal obsequies — dropping a deep curtsey each time they met — but otherwise kept her distance. During their infrequent and rather brittle *tête-à-têtes* about the Waleses' floundering marriage the Queen indicated that Diana's persistent bulimia was a cause, not a symptom, of their difficulties.

The Sovereign has also implied that the instability in their marriage is an over-riding consideration in any musings she may have about abdication. Naturally this does not please Prince Charles who refused to speak to his mother for several days following her 1991 Christmas broadcast when she spoke of her intention to serve the nation and the Commonwealth for "some years to come". For a man who holds his mother in total awe that silence was a measure of his anger. Once again he blamed the Princess of Wales. As he stalked along the corridors at Sandringham the Prince complained to anyone who would listen about the state of his marriage. Diana pointed out to him that he had already abdicated his regal responsibilities by allowing his brothers, Princes Andrew and Edward, to take over as counsellors of state, the official "stand ins" for the Sovereign when she is abroad on official business. If the Prince showed such indifference to these nominal constitutional duties, she asked sweetly, why should his mother give him the job.

Certainly the last twelve months have seen the Queen and daughter-in-law develop a more relaxed and cordial relationship. At a garden party last summer the Princess felt confident enough to essay a little joke about the Queen's black hat. She complimented her on the choice, remarking how it would come in useful for funerals. In a more serious vein they have had confidential discussions about her eldest son's state of mind. At times the Queen finds the direction of his life unfocused and his behaviour odd and erratic. It has not escaped her notice that he is as unhappy with his lot as his wife.

While Diana finds the monarchy as presently organized a crumbling institution, she has a deep respect for the manner in which the Queen has conducted herself for the last forty years. Indeed, much as she would like to leave her husband, Diana has emphasized to her: "I will never let you down." Before she attended a garden party on a stifling July afternoon last year, a friend offered Diana a fan to take with her. She refused saying: "I can't do that. My mother-in-law is going to be standing there with her handbag, gloves, stockings and shoes." It was a sentiment expressed in admiring tones for the Sovereign's complete self-control in every circumstance, however trying.

At the same time the Princess has had to adjust to other cross currents within the family. While Diana enjoys an amicable association with Prince Philip, whom she regards as a loner, she realizes that her husband is intimidated by his father. She accepts that his relationship with his eldest son is "tricky, very tricky". Charles longs to be patted on the back by his father while Prince Philip would like his son to consult him more frequently and at least recognize his contribution to public debate. It rankles with Prince Philip, for instance, that he started the discussion about the environment but it was Prince Charles who got the audience.

As with her father-in-law, Diana enjoys a distant but perfectly friendly relationship with her royal sister-in-law, the Princess Royal.

Diana appreciates at first hand the difficulties a royal woman faces within the organization and has nothing but admiration for her independence and endeavours, particularly on behalf of Save the Children Fund of which she is president. While their children often play together, Diana would never think to confide in the Princess or telephone her for lunch. She is pleased to see her when they meet at family occasions but that is as far as it goes. The media made a fuss at the time of Prince Harry's christening when Diana's decision not to choose Anne as a godparent was seen as a sign of their rancorous relations. The Princess was not asked simply because she was already an aunt to the boys and her role as godparent would merely duplicate matters. As with all the royal family, there will always be a divide between the two Princesses. Diana is an outsider by habit and inclination; Anne was born into the system. From time to time the Princess Royal has shown where her loyalties ultimately lie. A confrontation at Balmoral last year revealed the isolation of the two commoners, the Princess of Wales and the Duchess of York.

That confrontation on a warm August evening as the family enjoyed a barbecue in the grounds of Balmoral castle brought to the surface the nascent tensions and conflicts within their ranks. There was concern about an incident when Diana and Fergie had raced each other around the private roads in the Queen Mother's Daimler and a four-wheel drive estate vehicle. The argument became much more personal, focusing primarily on the Duchess of York. It resulted in her stalking off. Diana explained on Fergie's behalf that it was very difficult to marry into the royal family and that the Duchess was finding it harder the longer she stayed within their confines. She impressed upon the Queen the need to give the Duchess greater leeway, emphasizing that she was at the end of her tether. This was confirmed shortly afterwards by Fergie who told friends that 1991 was the last time she would visit Balmoral.

It was a vivid contrast with her first holiday at the Queen's summer retreat five years previously where she had so impressed the royal family with her enthusiasm and vigour. Over the years Diana has watched, often sympathetically, her sister-in-law being battered by the media and overwhelmed by the royal system which has gradually ground down her spirit. At times the floundering behaviour of the Duchess of York resembled not so much life imitating art but life imitating satire. As her clothes, her mothering instincts and her ill-chosen friends came in for caustic criticism, the Duchess turned to an assorted group of clairvoyants, tarot card readers, astrologers and other soothsayers to help her find a path through the royal maze. She was introduced to some by her friend Steve Wyatt, the adopted son of a Texan oil billionaire, but many she discovered for herself. Her frequent visits to Madame Vasso, a spiritualist who heals troubled minds and bodies by seating them under a blue plastic pyramid, were typical of the influences upon this increasingly restless and unhappy individual.

There were days when she had her fortune read and her astrological transits analysed every few hours. She tried to live her life by their predictions, her volatile spirit clinging to every scrap of solace in their musings. While Diana, like many members of the royal family, is interested and intrigued by the "New Age" approach to life, she is not ruled by every prophecy.

The Duchess however was held in their thrall, earnestly discussing their conclusions with her friends. The result was that over the last year the Duchess played Iago to Diana's Othello. She was an insistent voice in her ear, whispering, beseeching and imploring, at once predicting disaster and doom for the royal family while urging Diana to escape from the royal institution. It is no exaggeration to state

274

that barely a week passed last year without the Duchess of York discussing the latest portents with her sister-in-law and her close friends and advisers. In May 1991, when the marriage of the Prince and Princess of Wales came under renewed scrutiny, Fergie's "spooks" — as her friends describe them — predicted that Prince Andrew would soon become King and she the Queen.

While the Duke was excited by the prospect, his wife became increasingly disillusioned with her role. For a woman used to catching planes like others hail taxis, the claustrophobia of the royal world was more than she could bear. In August, her soothsayers forecast a problem involving a royal car, in September they said an imminent royal birth would create a crisis. Specific dates were mentioned but even when they passed without incident, the Duchess kept faith in her oracles. By November there was talk of a death in the family and as Diana prepared to spend Christmas at Sandringham with the royal family, she was warned by the Duchess that there would be a row between herself and Prince Charles. He would try to walk out but the Queen would stop him.

Interspersed with these dire portents, was the almost daily drip, drip, drip of pleading, reason and wish-fulfillment as the Duchess beseeched the Princess to join her and leave the royal family. Her invitation must have been an inviting prospect for a woman in an impossible position, but Diana has come to trust her own judgment.

In March 1992 the Duchess finally decided formally to separate from her husband and leave the royal family. The Princess watched the acrimonious collapse of her friend's marriage with sadness and alarm. She saw at first hand how quickly the Queen's courtiers could turn against her. They viciously attacked the Duchess, accusing her of behaving in a manner unbecoming of the royal family and cited various incidents when she had tried to profit from her royal associations. Courtiers even claimed, falsely, that the Duchess had hired a public relations company to publicize her departure from the royal family. As a BBC correspondent said: "The knives are out for the Duchess at Buckingham Palace." It was a foretaste of what Diana would have to endure if she decided to travel along that same road.

9

"I Did My Best"

A few days before the Queen celebrated the 40th anniversary of her accession, the Duke and Duchess of York drove from Buckingham Palace to Sandringham to see the Sovereign. On that bleak Wednesday in late January the royal couple formally discussed an issue which had troubled them for many months: their marriage. They had agreed that, after five years of married life, it would be sensible if they separated. The Duchess, as discussed earlier, had become increasingly disillusioned with her life within the royal family and depressed by continual and hurtful criticism, both inside and outside the palace, which showed no sign of abating. The final straw was the raucous discussion in the media about her relationship with Steve Wyatt, headlines provoked by the theft of photographs taken when the Duchess, Wyatt and others were on holiday in Morocco.

During that meeting at Sandringham the couple agreed to the Queen's suggestion that they should have a "cooling off" period of two months to allow time to reflect. Consequently the Duchess undertook only a couple of official engagements, spending the rest of the time with her family at Sunninghill Park or discussing her options with lawyers, members of the royal family, including the Princess of Wales and the Princess Royal, and close friends.

One of the first to be given the news was the Prince of Wales who was then staying on the Norfolk estate. He spoke to her about his own marriage difficulties, emphasizing that his constitutional position as direct heir to the throne made any thought of separation from Diana almost unthinkable. In a ringing rebuke the Duchess replied: "At least I've been true to myself." It is a sentiment which lies at the heart of the dilemma facing the Princess of Wales and strikes at the foundations of the modern monarchy.

The chronic instability of the marriage of the Prince and Princess of Wales and the collapse of Duke and Duchess of York's marriage is far more than a personal tragedy. It is a signal that a necessary experiment born of changed historical circumstances has failed. When George V granted permission for his son, the Duke of York, to marry a commoner, Lady Elizabeth Bowes-Lyon, he was recognizing the reality that the First World War had harvested European monarchies and dried up the supply of suitable royal brides and bridegrooms. It began the transition of a virtual royal caste, where royalty married royalty, to a class within society. But the grafting of commoners, however high born, onto the Hanoverian tree has been a disaster. Apart from the marriages of the present Queen and the Queen Mother, every significant union between royalty and commoner has ended in divorce, separation or an unwilling *status quo;* Princess Margaret and Antony Armstrong-Jones, Princess Anne and Captain Mark Phillips, the Duke and Duchess of York and the Prince and Princess of Wales. There is no obvious solution to the problem.

Is this state of affairs simply a reflection of the changing face of society or does it place a severe question mark about the way the royal family relate to outsiders? When Lady Diana Spencer wed Prince Charles, she also married into a family as welded in tradition and content in their insularity as any obscure South Sea island tribe. While their idiosyncrasies help shield them from the outside world, it also makes the task of a newcomer, who does not know the unspoken rules of the game, virtually impossible. The royal family is testimony to playwright Alan Bennett's maxim: "Every family has a secret and the secret is that it is not like any other family." The Queen and her sister, Princess Margaret, were the last generation immunized from reality. From an early age they have lived in palaces, absolutely cocooned from the outside world. The gilded cage has been their home and their life. A walk down the street, an afternoon's solitary shopping, waiting in line and making ends meet; these freedoms, however dubious, have never been part of their lives. For all their privileges, their squadrons of servants, their chauffeur-driven cars, private yachts and planes, they are prisoners of society's expectations and puppets of the system. Duty, obligation and sacrifice have been the expected and accepted threads of their lives and the weft and weave of the fabric of the Crown. The pursuit of personal happiness, as Princess Margaret discovered when she attempted to marry a divorcee, Group Captain Peter Townsend, has been sacrificed on the altar of monarchy and its moral ethos.

The Queen, groomed for the purple, has performed those traditional and expected functions of the Crown supremely well, so much so that she leaves an unattainable benchmark for her successor. The mould has been deliberately broken. As Lady Elizabeth Longford, the Queen's friend and biographer, has argued, one of the central achievements of the reign has been to educate her children in the real world. It has meant that her children are a hybrid generation, enjoying a taste of freedom but anchored to the world of castles and royal protocol. The actions, particularly of the Prince of Wales, demonstrate the particular perils of allowing future Sovereigns to breathe, even for a short time, the air of freedom. Unlike his predecessors, doubt, uncertainty and questioning have been added to his inherited faith in and acceptance of royal traditions.

Enter into this equation, then, the expectations and values of the commoners who have come into the family. It has proved an impossible hurdle to overcome. Lord Snowdon and Captain Mark Phillips were the first to fall, even though they had careers, photography and equestrian pursuits respectively, which took them outside the royal routine. The Princess of Wales and Duchess of York have enjoyed no such luxury. It is perhaps inevitable then that Diana, who watches the royal family from the inside, now sees a yawning gap between the way the world is moving and how it is perceived by the royal family. She believes that they are caught in an emotional timewarp without the necessary vision to appreciate the changes that have taken place in society. It was forcibly demonstrated during the royal family's traditional Christmas at

Sandringham this year. During dinner one evening, Diana tentatively raised the question of the future of the British monarchy in a federal Europe. The Queen, Prince Charles and the rest of the royal family looked at her as if she were mad and continued with their debate on who had shot the last pheasant of the day, a discussion which occupied the rest of the evening.

As a friend says: "She finds the monarchy claustrophobic and completely outdated with no relevance to today's life and problems. She feels that it is a crumbling institution and believes that the family won't know what has hit it in a few years' time unless it changes too."

Diana has discussed with her counsellor Stephen Twigg these serious doubts about the existing foundations of the monarchy. He argues: "If the royal family doesn't change and their relationships with the rest of society don't change, it is on a hiding to nothing. It can only deteriorate as a useful organ of society. It must remain dynamic and respond to changes. It's not just the royal family who must change but society itself must examine the way it looks at the royal family. Do we want the royal family to be revered because of their position or in a modern society do we want to admire them because of the way they cope with the traumas of everyday life and learn from them in the process?"

Although Diana has successfully shaken off the traditional image of the fairy-tale princess concerned exclusively with shopping and fashion it still colours the preconceptions of those she meets for the first time. She is used to being patronized. As she tells close friends: "It happens a lot. It's interesting to see people's reactions to me. They have one impression in mind and then, as they talk to me, I can see it changing." At the same time her struggles within the royal family have made her realize that she must not hide behind the conventional mask of monarchy. The spontaneity, the tactile compassion and the generosity of spirit she displays in public are very genuine. It is not an act for public consumption. The Princess, who appreciates how the royal world anaesthetizes individuals from reality, is fiercely determined that her boys are prepared for the outside world in a way unknown to previous royal generations. Normally royal children are trained to hide their feelings and emotions from others, constructing a shield to deflect intrusive inquiry. Diana believes that William and Harry should be open and honest to the possibilities within themselves and the variety of approaches to understanding life. As she says: "I want to

283

bring them up with security. I hug my children to death and get into bed with them at night. I always feed them love and affection, it's so important."

The cultural code of the stiff upper lip is not for her boys. She is teaching them that it is not "sissy" to show their feelings to others. When she took Prince William to watch the German tennis star Steffi Graff win the women's singles final at Wimbledon last year they left the royal box to go backstage and congratulate her on her victory. As Graff walked off court down the dimly lit corridor to the dressing room, royal mother and son thought Steffi looked so alone and vulnerable out of the spotlight. So first Diana, then William, gave her a kiss and an affectionate hug.

The way the Princess introduced her boys to her dying friend, Adrian Ward-Jackson, was a practical lesson in seeing the reality of life and death. When Diana told her eldest son that Adrian had died, his instinctive response revealed his maturity. "Now he's out of pain at last and really happy." At the same time the Princess is acutely aware of the added burdens of rearing two boys who are popularly known as "the heir and the spare." Self-discipline is part of the training. Every night at six o'clock the boys sit down and write thank-you notes or letters to friends and family. It is a discipline which Diana's father instilled in her, so much so that if she returns from a dinner party at midnight she will not sleep easily unless she has penned a letter of thanks.

William and Harry, now ten and nearly eight respectively, are now aware of their destiny. On one occasion the boys were discussing their futures with Diana. "When I grow up I want to be a policeman and look after you mummy," said William lovingly. Quick as a flash Harry replied, with a note of triumph in his voice, "Oh no you can't, you've got to be king."

As their uncle, Earl Spencer, says their characters are very different from the public image. "The press have always written up William as the terror and Harry as a rather quiet second son. In fact William is a very self-possessed, intelligent and mature boy and quite shy. He is quite formal and stiff, sounding older than his years when he answers the phone." It is Harry who is the mischievous imp of the family. Harry's puckish character manifested itself to his uncle during the return flight from Necker, the Caribbean island owned by Virgin airlines boss Richard Branson. He recalls: "Harry was presented with his breakfast. He had his headphones on and a computer game in front of him but he was determined to eat his croissant. It took him about five minutes to manoeuvre all his electronic gear, his knife, his croissant and his butter. When he eventually managed to get a mouthful there was a look of such complete satisfaction on his face. It was a really wonderful moment."

His godparent Carolyn Bartholomew says, without an ounce of prejudice, that Harry is "the most affectionate, demonstrative and huggable little boy" while William is very much like his mother, "intuitive, switched on and highly perceptive". At first she thought the future king was a "little terror". "He was naughty and had tantrums," she recalls. "But when I had my two children I realized that they are all like that at some point. In fact William is kind-hearted, very much like Diana. He would give you his last Rolo sweet. In fact he did on one occasion. He was longing for this sweet, he only had one left and he gave it to me." Further evidence of his generous heart occurred when he gathered together all his pocket money, which only amounted to a few pence, and solemnly handed it over to her.

But he is no angel as Carolyn saw when she visited Highgrove. Diana had just finished a swim in the open air pool and had changed into a white towelling dressing gown as she waited for William to follow her. Instead he splashed about as though he were drowning and slowly sank to the bottom. His mother, not knowing whether it was a fake or not, struggled to get out of her robe. Then, realizing the urgency, she dived in still in her dressing gown. At that moment he resurfaced, shouting and laughing at the success of his ruse. Diana was not amused.

Generally William is a youngster who displays qualities of responsibility and thoughtfulness beyond his years and enjoys a close rapport with his younger brother whom friends believe will make an admirable adviser behind the scenes when William eventually becomes king. Diana feels that it is a sign that in some way they will share the burdens of monarchy in the years to come. Her approach is conditioned by her firmly held belief that she will never become queen and that her husband will never become King Charles III.

The boys have been a loving lifeline for the Princess in her isolated position. "They mean everything to me," she is fond of saying. However, in September this year, when Prince Harry joins his elder brother at Ludgrove preparatory school, Diana will have to face the prospect of an empty nest at Kensington Palace. "She realizes that they are gong to develop and expand and that soon a chapter in her own life will be complete," observes James Gilbey.

The loss of her boys, at least during term time, will only serve to highlight her cruel predicament — especially as the Duchess of York has already left the royal scene. Diana's world may be characterized as an unstable equilibrium; the unhappiness of her marriage balanced by the satisfaction she finds in her royal work, particularly among the sick and the dying; the suffocating certainties of the royal system matched by her growing self-confidence in using the organization for the benefit of her work.

Her thinking about her royal position changes by the month. However, while the graph of her progress shows various ups and downs, the general trend over the past year has been towards staying within rather than leaving the organization. She now feels impatience with the creaking machinery of monarchy rather than despair, business-like indifference towards Prince Charles as opposed to shrinking deference and cool disregard of Camilla Parker-Bowles rather than jealous rage. It is by no means a consistent development but her growing interest in how to control and reform the system as well as her serious committment to use her position to do good in the world point to staying rather than taking flight. At the same time the Duchess's departure merely adds another element of uncertainty in an already precarious position.

It is not an issue for complacency. The Princess can be a volatile, impatient young woman whose moods regularly swing from optimism to despair. As astrologer Felix Lyle says: "She is prone to depression, a woman who is easily defeated and dominated by those with a strong character. Diana has a self-destructive side. At any moment she could say 'to hell with the lot of you' and go off. The potential is there. She is a flower waiting to bud."

One evening she can be immensely mature, discussing death and the after-life with George Carey, the new Archbishop of Canterbury, the next night giggling away at a bridge party. "Sometimes she is possessed by a different spirit in response to breaking free from the yoke of responsibility that binds her," observed Rory Scott who still sees the Princess socially.

As her brother says: "She has done very well to keep her sense of humour, that is what relaxes people around her. She is not at all stuffy and will make a joke happily either about herself or about something ridiculous which everyone has noticed but is too embarrassed to talk about." Royal tours, these outdated exercises in stultifying boredom and ancient ceremonial, are rich seams for her finely tuned sense of the ridiculous. After a day watching native dancers in unbearable humidity or sipping a cup of some foul-tasting liquid, she often telephones her friends to regale them with the latest absurdities. "The things I do for England," is her favourite phrase. She was particularly tickled when she asked the Pope about his "wounds" during a private audience in the Vatican shortly after he had been shot. He thought she was talking about her "womb" and congratulated her on her impending new arrival. While her instinct and intuition are finely honed, "She understands the essence of people, what a person is about rather than who they are," says her friend Angela Serota — Diana recognizes that her intellectual hinterland needs development. The girl who left school without an "O" level to her name now harbours a quiet ambition to study psychology and mental health. "Anything to do with people," she says.

Although she has a tendency to be overly impressed by those with academic qualifications, Diana admires people who perform rather than pontificate. Richard Branson, the head of Virgin airlines, Baron Jacob Rothschild, the millionaire banker who restored Spencer House, and her cousin Viscount

David Linley who runs a successful furniture and catering business, are high on her list. "She likes the fact that David has been able to break out of the royal mould and do something positive," says a friend. "She envies too his good fortune in being able to walk down a street without a detective."

For years her low intellectual self-esteem manifested itself in instinctive deference towards the judgments of her husband and senior courtiers. Now that she is clearer herself about her direction, she is prepared to argue about policy in a way that would have been unthinkable several years ago. The results are tangible. Foreign Office diplomats, notoriously hidebound in their perceptions, are beginning to realize her true worth. They were impressed by the way she handled her first solo visit to Pakistan and subsequently discussed trips to Egypt and Iran, the Islamic republic where the Union Jack was routinely burned until a few years ago. This is, as she would say, a "very grown-up" part of her royal life.

The speeches she is making with almost weekly regularity are a further satisfying feature of her royal life. Some she writes herself, others by a small coterie of advisers, including her private secretary Patrick Jephson, now a firm ally in the royal camp as she personally appointed him last November. It is a flexible informal group who discuss with the Princess the points she wants to make, research the statistics and then construct the speech.

The contrast between her real interests and the role assigned for her by her palace "minders" was amply demonstrated in March this year where on the same day she was guest of honour at the Ideal Home Exhibition and in the evening made a passionate and revelatory speech about AIDS. There was an interesting symbolism to these engagements, separated only by a matter of hours but by a generation in personal philosophy. Her exhibition visit was organized by the palace bureaucracy. They arranged everything from photo opportunities to guests lists while the subsequent media coverage concentrated on an off-the-cuff remark the Princess made about how she couldn't comment on her plans for National Bed Week because this was "a family show". It was light, bright and trite, the usual offering which is served up by the palace to the media day in day out. The Princess performed her role impeccably, chatting to the various organizers and smiling for the cameras. However her performance was just that, a role which the palace, the media and public have come to expect.

A glimpse of the real Diana was on show

later that evening when in the company of Professor Michael Adler and Margaret Jay, both AIDS experts, she spoke to an audience of media executives at a dinner held at Claridges. Her speech clearly came from the heart and her own experience. Afterwards she answered several rather long-winded questions from the floor, the first occasion in her royal life where she had subjected herself to this particular ordeal. This episode passed without a murmur in the media even though it represented a significant milestone in her life. It illustrates the considerable difficulties she faces in shifting perceptions of her job as a Princess, both inside and outside the palace walls.

These days her family, particularly her sisters, Jane and Sarah, and brother Charles, are aware of the appalling problems she has endured. Jane has always given sensible advice and Sarah, from being dubious of her kid sister's success, is now very protective. "You never criticize Diana in front of her," notes a friend. Her relations with her mother and her father, when he was alive, are patchier. While Diana enjoys a sporadic but affectionate relationship with her mother, she was robust in her reaction to news that her second husband, Peter Shand Kydd, had left her for another woman. Last summer her bond with her father went through a difficult period following publicity surrounding the secret sale of treasures from Althorp House. The children, including the Princess, had written to their father objecting to the trade in family heirlooms. There were bitter exchanges, subsequently regretted, which deeply hurt the Princess of Wales. Even the Prince of Wales intervened, voicing his concern to Raine Spencer who was typically robust in her response. Last autumn a reconciliation between father and daughter was effected. During a leisurely tour around the world the late Earl Spencer was deeply touched by the affection shown towards his youngest daughter by so many strangers. He telephoned from America to tell her just how proud of her that made him feel.

The support of her family is matched by the encouragement of the small group of friends and counsellors who see the real Diana, not the glowing image presented for public consumption. They are under no illusions that, while the Princess is a woman of considerable virtues, her character is prone to pessimism and despair, qualities which increase the likelihood of her leaving the system. The departure of the Duchess of York from the royal scene has exacerbated that defeatist side of her personality.

As she has admitted to friends: "Everyone

said I was the Marilyn Monroe of the 1980s and I was adoring every minute of it. Actually I've never sat down and said: 'Hooray how wonderful.' Never. The day I do we're in trouble. I am performing a duty as the Princess of Wales as long as my time is allocated but I don't see it any longer than fifteen years."

While she has the right to feel sorry for herself, all too often this spills over into self-imposed martyrdom. As James Gilbey says: "When she is confident she extends herself and pushes out the barriers. As soon as there is a chink in the armour she immediately retreats away from the fray." At times it is almost as though she wants to engineer a hurt or a rejection before she is deserted by those she trusts and loves. This has resulted in her blocking out her allies at crucial periods in her royal life when she has most needed support.

As the Princess performs the impossible balancing act which her life requires, she drifts inexorably into obsession, continually discussing her problems. Her friend Carolyn Bartholomew argues it is difficult not to be self-absorbed when the world watches everything she does. "How can you not be self-obsessed when half the world is watching everything you do; the high-pitched laugh when someone is talking to somebody famous must make you very very cynical." She endlessly debates the problems she faces in dealing with her husband, the royal family, and their system. They remain tantalizingly unresolved, the gulf between thought and action achingly great. Whether she stays or goes, the example of the Duchess of York is a potent source of instability. James Gilbey sums up Diana's dilemma: "She can never be happy unless she breaks away but she won't break away unless Prince Charles does it. He won't do it because of his mother so they are never going to be happy. They will continue under the farcical umbrella of the royal family yet they will both lead completely separate lives."

Her friend Carolyn Bartholomew, a sensible sounding-board throughout Diana's adult life, sees how that fundamental issue has clouded her character. "She is kind, generous, sad and in some ways rather desperate. Yet she has maintained her self-deprecating sense of humour. A very shrewd but immensely sorrowful lady."

Her royal future is by no means well-defined. If she could write her own script the Princess would like to see her husband go off with his Highgrove friends and attempt to discover the happiness he has not found with her, leaving Diana free to groom Prince William for his eventual destiny as the Sovereign.

It is an idle pipe-dream as impossible as Prince Charles's wish to relinquish his regal position and run a farm in Italy. She has other more modest ambitions; to spend a weekend in Paris, take a course in psychology, learn the piano to concert grade and to start painting again. The current pace of her life makes even these hopes seem grandiose, never mind her oft-repeated vision of the future where she see herself one day settling abroad, probably in Italy or France. A more likely avenue is the unfolding vista of charity, community and social work which has given her a sense of self-worth and fulfillment. As her brother says: "She has got a strong character. She does know what she wants and I think that after ten years she has got to a plateau now which she will continue to occupy for many years."

As a child she sensed her special destiny, as an adult she has remained true to her instincts. Diana has continued to carry the burden of public expectations while enduring considerable personal problems. Her achievement has been to find her true self in the face of overwhelming odds. She will continue to tread a different path from her husband, the royal family and their system and yet still conform to their traditions. As she says: "When I go home and turn my light off at night, I know I did my best."

Appendix
Could Charles and
Diana divorce?

What are the present divorce laws?

The present divorce laws are embodied in the Divorce Reform Act 1969 which came into force in 1971, and the Matrimonial Causes Act 1973. The sole ground for divorce is now "the irretrievable breakdown of a marriage", but this may be evidenced by reference to one or more of five facts. These are: adultery, unreasonable behaviour, two years' desertion, two years' separation with the respondent's consent to divorce, and five years' separation, regardless of the respondent's consent.

The Matrimonial Causes Act also embodies the division of property on a divorce between the parties, which in a royal divorce could lead to some difficult decisions.

Charles and Diana are subjects of the United Kingdom and therefore could petition for divorce like everyone else. Recent years have seen the divorce of the Earl of Harewood, the

Queen's first cousin, who was divorced in 1967 under the previous divorce laws, and Princess Margaret who was legally separated and then divorced. Princess Anne has also recently filed for divorce.

What would be the title of the Princess of Wales following a divorce?

This would of course be subject to decisions by the Queen and Privy Council, and would depend on the original causes of the divorce. There seems no reason why she should not maintain the title of Princess but this would probably be conditional on her not marrying again. There are foreign precedents in the cases of Princess Muna of Jordan, the second wife of King Hussein, and Princess Soraya of Iran, the second Queen or Empress of the last Shah.

What would be the position of the children, Princes William and Harry?

Their position as heirs would be unaffected. They would still stand as second and third in succession to the throne.

Could Prince Charles marry again?

He could marry again, but whether he could succeed to the throne after a divorce and re-marriage is another question.

Following his divorce he would have to ask the permission of the Queen to remarry, under the Royal Marriages Act, 1772. If the Queen refused her permission, then he could, under the Act, serve notice to the Privy Council that he intended to marry without the Sovereign's consent. Only both Houses of Parliament could then prevent a valid marriage taking place.

In practice, this second possibility has never occurred, and if there is any difficulty then this is usually resolved by negotiations outside the strict legal framework, either between the Queen and the Prime Minister, or, in a wider context, after consultation with the Commonwealth Prime Ministers. This happened in 1936, when informal soundings at least were taken over the matrimonial difficulties of Edward VIII and again in 1955 when Princess Margaret wished to marry the divorced Group Captain Townsend.

A marriage abroad has sometimes been a solution. This took place in the cases of both the Earl of Harewood and Prince Michael of Kent, the first marrying in Gibraltar and the second in Vienna.

In order to be able to marry again, Prince Charles would probably have to give up his rights to the throne and to the succession. This was suggested to Princess Margaret in 1955. She was not willing to do this, as she was then third in succession to the throne.

Officially the Church of England does not approve of divorce, and as the Sovereign is Supreme Governor of the Church of England, it would be extremely difficult for a Sovereign to give permission for the heir to marry again having been divorced. Secondly, it would pose serious difficulties if a divorced person were to succeed to the throne or if the Sovereign were to consider marrying a divorcee. In 1936 the then Archbishop of Canterbury warned Edward VIII that he would probably not be able to crown him if he married a divorcee.

Any second marriage by Prince Charles would almost certainly be only a civil marriage, and therefore probably not recognised by the church. However, some sovereigns have been divorced *after* being crowned.

A divorced person has never succeeded to the throne in this country with the sole exception of George I.

Could Princess Diana marry again?
She could, but she would almost certainly then forfeit her title of Royal Highness and Princess, and probably any regular income or settlement which she had obtained at the

301

time of the divorce.

What would be the position of a second wife of Prince Charles?

As it is a principle in England that a woman shares the titles of her husband, then as he is a Prince by birth, his second wife would become a Princess. Whether she would become Princess of Wales would depend on whether he himself would have the title if he was no longer considered eligible for the throne by reason of the divorce.

There is the precedent of Buckingham Palace intervening and preventing the title of Princess being acquired by Wallis Warfield on her marriage to the Duke of Windsor in 1937, but there are many legal experts who have questioned the legitimacy of this move.

What would be the position of any children born of Prince Charles's second marriage?

They would be Princes or Princesses as they take the title of their father and would take their place in the order of succession after Princes William and Harry and their issue. There is not, legally, any such thing as a morganatic marriage in England, although there have been such in practical terms, for example the marriages of the Dukes of Sussex and

Cambridge in the last century.

What income would Princess Diana have if divorced?
This would depend on the parties themselves and their lawyers working out a settlement, as in any other divorce. There would be unique royal problems, such as the wealth of presents they received on their marriage, and the homes and possessions they have acquired during their marriage. Diana would almost certainly be given a substantial property of her own and a house in London, and possibly two incomes: one for life, as the mother of two heirs to the throne, and one which she would forfeit if she married again.

Would Diana be able to carry out any royal duties after a divorce?
This is highly unlikely, as it would prejudice the position of any new wife of Prince Charles. However, it is possible that she could carry out duties with her two young sons while they are still under-age, and she could continue as patroness of any institution or cause which she has espoused as Princess of Wales.

Lord Snowdon and Mark Phillips have not carried out any official duties since divorce or separation, although Snowdon has been personally invited by the Queen as photog-

303

rapher on a number of royal occasions subsequent to the divorce.

Michael Nash
Lecturer in law
Norwich City College
April 1992